MINIBIKES AND SMALL CYCLES

About the Book

Climb aboard a minibike or small cycle and ride into a different world of freedom and adventure. In this book the well-known writer Irwin Stambler shows how today's lightweight cycles pack a lot of punch in small packages. These lightweights can take you any number of places you couldn't go in a car or would care to try on a bicycle. Mr. Stambler offers an up-to-date view of the great variety of minibikes and small cycles now on the market. He gives excellent tips on how to pick the one that's right for you, how to keep it serviced, and—above all—to remember that safety is the prime rule for every cyclist.

IRWIN STAMBLER

MINIBIKES
AND
SMALL
CYCLES

G. P. Putnam's Sons, New York

Photo Credits

Goodyear, pp. 55, 90, 111 and 112
Honda, pp. 33 and 73
Kawasaki, pp. 13, 14, 17, 23, 49, 51, 67, 88, 105, 106 and 108
Suzuki, p. 83
Yamaha, pp. 40 and 79

Copyright © 1977 by Irwin Stambler
All rights reserved. Published
simultaneously in Canada by
Longman Canada Limited, Toronto.
Printed in the United States of America
10 up

Library of Congress Cataloging in Publication Data
Stambler, Irwin
Minibikes and small cycles
Includes index.
Summary: Discusses the purchase, service, and safe
operation of minibikes and lightweight cycles.
1. Minibikes—Juvenile literature. 2. Minicycles—
Juvenile literature. [1. Minibikes. 2. Minicycles]
I. Title.
TL443.S75   1977   629.22'75   76-25174
ISBN 0-399-20566-7
ISBN 0-399-61055-3 lib. bdg.
Second Impression

CONTENTS

1
PLEASURE IN SMALL PACKAGES

Air caresses your face and swirls around your helmet. Under a bright sky the sun glints dazzlingly from polished chrome and brightly painted metal. You sense the rapid answer of the wheels to the surge of power from the engine as you twist the throttle. There's a feeling of freedom as you ride a small motorcycle.

With a minibike or a lightweight cycle, you can transport yourself into a different world. For many of these lightweight machines the word *small* applies only in relationship to big, costly two-wheelers. Today's lightweight cycles pack a lot of punch in small packages. Even the smallest minibike designed for a preteener can do things some full-size cycles could not do five to ten years ago. The engines for lightweights are compact but efficient: Pound for pound they are several times more effective than the engine in a big modern car.

Those lightweights can take you any number of places you couldn't go in a car or would care to try on a bicycle. You can't drive a car through some of the narrow alleyways between local buildings or take a spin around the backyard for practice. Cars and bicycles can't get around some of the dusty winding trails in the backcountry that are no problem for off-road type motorcycles. And they can't flash up and down some of the hills or slopes that provide excitement and challenges for riders of small cycles.

But even if you could drive a car or take a train or bus to some places, it's not the same as using a cycle. With your helmet snapped snugly in place, your hands gripping the handlebars, and knees pressed close against the frame, you're in a special world of your own, free to think your own thoughts. It's this oneness with the bike and the rider's innermost feelings that is one of the lures of cycling for a growing number of people of all ages.

For some, of course, an equally important incentive is the thought of competition, of a feeling of association with the pulse-pounding thrills of motocross, TTs or other types of racing. As a spectator at professional events, you get added insight from your own riding experience. Even though you're of elementary or high school age you can imagine yourself a champ like Gary Nixon or Kenny Roberts while taking part in specially supervised minibike or small-cycle races set up by national motorcycle organizations. You do not have to be a skyscraping specimen or a heavy-muscled type to be a success at cycle racing. An example is Dave Aldana, 5 feet 4 inches and weighing only 145 pounds, who became one of the top riders in the early 1970s. His career started with a lightweight cycle. As he told an interviewer, "When I was about fourteen, my dad bought me a Suzuki eighty and I did a lot of riding out in the desert around Perris and Elsinore (in Southern California). My dad rode in scrambles, and I went along with him."

Kenny Roberts, the motorcycle racer with the most victories in the mid-1970s, also is slight in build. In fact, while growing up in Tennessee on his father's horse farm, he was urged to become a jockey. As he told Shav Glick of the Los Angeles *Times,* "A lot of friends tried to talk me into it, but before I could try, I had my first ride on a motorcycle. That did it. Horses have minds of their own. They want to go where they want. Motorcycles don't have a mind. They go where you want them to. And a heck of a lot faster, too."

This doesn't mean that only people of average height or less can do well in racing. Record books show champions of every shape, size, and gender. The point is that the premium is on technique and reflexes, not necessarily physical advantages. The powered two-wheeler is a great equalizer.

Not that speed is all that important for enjoment of cycling. In fact, most cycles have only moderate speed compared to other forms of powered transportation. (But they are many times faster and provide much greater flexibility than a bicycle.)

A pro rider like Don Smith can do a lot of tricks with a motorcycle, the result of years of experience that often begins with small cycle riding.

After you've mastered the art of riding a small cycle, you'll get an extra thrill knowing what goes into the mastery of expert riders like world champion motorcycle jumper Bob Gill.

Gary Gabelich, in the mid-1970s called the "fastest man on wheels," set a record of 622.407 miles per hour (MPH) in the Blue Flame rocket car and may become the first person to exceed the speed of sound on land. But he gets as much thrill out of taking a long ride on his motorcycle at only 40 or 50 MPH.

"I learned to ride a motorcycle when I was in my teens," he says. "It was one of my most exciting 'firsts' and I never lost my love for it. I enjoy getting out in the backcountry and looking at the landscape or seeing some of the wildlife. Or I get pleasure from taking out my cycle in the evening to go riding along the Southern California coastline around Palos Verdes. It's a very good feeling, one of being at peace with the world and with yourself."

Perhaps the nicest thing about minibikes and small cycles is that they come in such a range of sizes and capabilities. Whether you're old or young, short or tall, there's a model that should suit your needs. Most important, there are many well-designed lightweight cycles that don't cost much. There are bikes priced well under $200 that can offer a lot of performance for a novice or an experienced rider.

You say you've got more money to spend. You want a bike with more horsepower, a five- or ten-speed gearbox, a bigger fuel tank? No problem! The array of models on the market in minibikes and lightweights provides anything a cycle fan could want for just about any use from a limited street bike to a motocross racer.

One major attraction of these cycles is the progress they represent over the designs of a decade or two ago. In those days you didn't see too many people riding cycles because it took a lot of time, money and dedication to master the large, heavy models. It took a while for motorcycle designers to realize just how popular bikes could become if they were made simpler to operate, store or transport than the old style machines. Once cycle engineers—and particularly Japanese experts—understood this, they turned things around in a short time. You can see what happened by comparing some of the sleek, efficient models on dealers' floors with some of the huge two-wheelers still favored by stunt riders and some police officers.

At first the new lightweights were essentially stripped down versions of full-size, high-powered cycles. After a while designers began to devise streamlined bikes powered by increasingly more powerful engines that

15

formed a whole new class of two-wheelers. As a glance around the streets reveals, this cycle revolution has made the lightweight a truly universal system. As a result, increasing numbers of people have discovered the pleasures of cycling. It is reflected in current sales figures showing that the majority of new cycles sold are in the small and medium categories (under 600 cubic centimeters [cc] engine displacement) rather than large touring machines. And the trend seems to be toward wider use of cycles classified as lightweight rather than the high end of the "medium" class.

(*Engine displacement* is a technical term, one of a number you will become familiar with as you get into the basis of cycling. It means the volume available in the engine cylinder when the piston is at the low point of its motion.)

An understanding of how motorcycles work and a general familiarity with different types of cycles are important if you are to make a wise choice of the "wheels" you're going to use. If you're like a great many cycle enthusiasts, you'll want to go beyond that, literally to the nuts and bolts level. Tinkering with a machine like this and solving operating problems on your own can provide a lot of satisfaction as well as an impressive savings in money. Another happy attribute of most modern lightweights is their excellent design so that someone wanting to do the maintenance work at home can accomplish most of it without trouble.

Separating motorcycles on the basis of engine displacement can be misleading, of course, as we'll see later. For instance, in trying to define what is meant by a minibike, experts at first set down a maximum engine displacement of 45–50 cc as one of the guidelines. When this proved too low, they suggested a limit of 99 cc. But a look at minibike catalogs of today shows that there are cycles classed as minibikes with engines boasting displacements up to 200 cc.

One generality applicable to most minibikes is that they are designed primarily for limited off-road use. The majority of makes should never be ridden in the street, but rather in backyards, vacant lots, or places set aside for bike riding. In keeping with this concept, most models are built for ease of transportation away from congested areas. Many have folddown handlebars and fold-up footpegs so you can fit them easily into a car trunk or the back of a station wagon. They are light enough so you don't have to get sore muscles lifting them into such storage areas.

In the interest of keeping the price low and providing the utmost

16

A proud owner shows off his small cycle—a Kawasaki MC-1M dirt bike.

simplicity for beginning riders, many minibikes engineers cut back on performance and on equipment that would be required for intensive operation. On the other hand, small cycles—many of them having motors with ratings similar to those used on minibikes—are being produced with capabilities needed for legal use on city streets or with the ruggedness demanded for extensive off-road cycling. But it must be emphasized again that some minibikes offer performance to delight riders with considerable experience.

Enjoyment and adventure are good reasons for wanting a small cycle, but there are some other strong arguments as well. For example, consider the need to conserve energy resources and the environment. Using a motorcycle instead of a car for leisure or for transportation can help both.

Many studies conducted by cycle companies indicate that the more people switch from the auto to the motorcycle the less pollutants go into the air. One such survey, taken in the mid-1970s, indicated the 7 to 8 million cycles in use in the United States contributed only 0.9 percent of hydrocarbon emissions, only 0.6 percent of carbon monoxide, 0.5 percent of solid particles and just 0.03 percent of nitrogen oxides. Of course, bicycles are completely pollution free, but in powered vehicles, motorcycle engineers claim, nothing comes close to the lightweight two-wheeler. As one of them points out, "Even doubling the number of motorcycles in use in this country would not cause a significant increase in the overall level of pollutants. And work is continuing on emission control devices for new motorcycle engines that will do an even more impressive job."

In the mid-seventies, there was some controversy about the pollution performance of cycles. Some environmentalists claimed they had run tests showing motorcycles were actually quite "dirty." Industry experts, though, felt their data were valid. A Honda spokesman stressed, "So far [as of mid-'76] none of those investigators has identified such things as what controls were used, whether bikes were large or small, old or new, etc. Our engineers state we already meet or better Environmental Protection Agency pollution levels and we can meet or better EPA requirements more stringent than currently set for cars."

As fuel becomes harder to get and more expensive, motorcycles look more attractive, particularly lightweights, because their fuel economy is superior to their larger brothers'.

Fuel economy relates to weight. The more weight an engine must move around, the more fuel it will burn to move a vehicle a given distance. This is why government experts urge wider use of small cars to save valuable fuel supplies. The same thing applies to motorcycles: the lighter the cycle, the less fuel needed to run it. Thus most small and medium cycles can get 60, 70 and, in many cases, over 100 miles per gallon while the big 650- or 750-cc designs offer 20–40 miles per gallon. This situation is naturally reflected in fuel tank size. The big boys have capacities of from three to six gallons, while the small cycles and minis do the job with tanks holding only one or two gallons.

This is nice to know when you see the price of gasoline moving skyward. Even at prices of 60 or 70 cents a gallon, you can do a lot of traveling on a lightweight. By comparison, it would cost $2 to $3 to cover the same territory on a large motorcycle. So not only can you have a lot of fun for very little money riding a small cycle, you also have the knowledge that you're helping conserve a precious resource.

In fact, if friends or relatives seem to think using a motorcycle instead of a car is a form of self-indulgence, you can quote impressive statistics on what this means in terms of energy conservation. Kawasaki engineers note, "Driving 21 miles per day, about 500 miles per month, a car which averages 15 miles per gallon consumes only 13.3 gallons per month. However, if 500,000 drivers were to switch from cars to motorcycles, the fuel saving would be 13,350,000 gallons per month. The yearly saving would be a staggering 160,200,000 gallons." These figures are for medium- and larger-size bikes. If the same number of people switched to small cycles, savings of over 300,000,000 gallons a year might be achieved.

If you're new to motorcycling, you might think the rising popularity of the powered two-wheeler represents a new step in transportation. Actually, as a brief look at cycle history shows, the motorcycle came along before the automobile. The first cars weren't called cars or automobiles, but *motocycles* (without the *r*). At the time, any engine-driven street vehicle was referred to in that way.

The motorcycle obviously is descended from the bicycle and all the early ones were essentially bicycles with an engine replacing the pedals for motive power. The first powered bike is attributed to W. W. Austin of Winthrop, Massachusetts, who built it in 1866. The gasoline-fueled internal combustion engine, the device you'll be concerned with as a devoted cycle fan, had been suggested (by the Frenchman Beau de Rochas in 1862), but not demonstrated. So the Austin design was steam-driven. The steam boiler was suspended back of the seat and the expanding steam moved piston rods back and forth that were directly connected to the rear wheel.

A truly practical steam-run bike wasn't developed, so the powered two-wheeler didn't have much public impact until the internal-combustion engine came into existence. Professor Nikolaus Otto in Germany made the first dramatic breakthrough when he demonstrated a four-stroke-cycle internal-combustion engine in 1877. A co-worker named Gottlieb Daimler went out on his own in the early 1880s and started building four-stroke engines in a shop in Bad Kannstadt, Germany. The story goes that his son came in one day tired from a ride on his bicycle and Daimler thought of fitting the bike with an engine. The result was a rather unwieldy two-wheeler using a large powerplant with a displacement of 264 cc and a top speed hardly higher than that of a bicycle. But, as Daimler's son showed on November 10, 1885, it worked.

Soon improved internal combusion engines appeared both in Europe and the United States, and eager inventors began proposing schemes for all kinds of vehicles. Many of these were just regular bicycles rigged to use an engine. By the turn of the century, though, motorcycle pioneers had come to realize that an efficiently powered two-wheeler could only be gained by starting out with a design based on engine requirements. The motorized bike needed wheels with different dimensions and tire configurations, saddle heights generally closer to the ground than for bikes and, in particular, a different weight distribution than for a bicycle.

By the early 1900s high quality engine-driven two wheelers, looking much like those used today, were coming off production lines in the United States and Europe. The United States became an early leader in the field. The famous Indian motorcycle, developed by bike racer Carl Oscar Hedstrom and built for decades in Springfield, Massachusetts, appeared in 1901 and swiftly became the motorcycle equivalent of Henry Ford's Model T. In the first two decades dozens of motorcycle companies flourished in the United States.

As the automobile became the favored form of transportation in America, however, the ferment of the early 1900s faded, and little was done to improve the basic cycle design. Cycle production in the United States dwindled, and only a few companies were still operating after World War II. Meanwhile, the motorcycle prospered elsewhere. England became a major producer of excellent cycles in the decades between the two World Wars. After World War II, the economic resurgence in Japan, combined with the limited incomes of most Japanese, catapulted the engine-driven two-wheeler to prominence in that country. The man who almost single-handedly accomplished that is a onetime automobile repair-shop operator named Soichiro Honda.

Born in a rural village near the city of Hamamatsu in 1906, Honda, the son of a blacksmith, was caught up in the same excitement about science and technology that caused American boys to grow up to help make the United States the foremost industrial power in the world. This interest took hold almost as soon as he could understand what was going on around him.

"If I remember correctly," he told an interviewer, "it was at the age of four or five that I first began to take an interest in engines. There was a rice-milling plant a few miles from my home, and it had a diesel engine which fascinated me. I watched it endlessly as the engine operated in a cloud of exhaust fumes and a clatter of noise. When I was in the second grade, the first motor car came to our village. It had a folding roof, and I followed it hastily. When the car stopped, it leaked a considerable amount of oil on the ground. The smell of oil has always enchanted me, and I literally put my nose to the ground and breathed in deeply."

Honda began as an automobile mechanic and later was a motorcycle and auto racer. He progressed from that to owner of a company that made piston rings for the Japanese World War II war effort. After the war he sold the plant and dabbled with various inventions until he saw the chance to buy 500 government-surplus small engines. He got the idea of using them to power bicycles. Transportation of any kind was scarce at the time, and people eagerly bought his inventory.

No more surplus engines were available, so Honda designed his own single-cylinder, 50-cc engine, called the "chimney engine" because of the odd stuck-out-on-top shape of the cylinder head. A modified version, called the A-type, which produced a half horsepower, was soon in production, and Honda Motor Company, Ltd., was in business. The motorized bike it powered did so well, the company developed the first true Honda motorcycles. Most notable of these was the D-type "Dream" powered by a new 100-cc two-cycle, single-cylinder engine that developed 2.3 horsepower. Significantly, Honda and his co-workers were refining small but powerful engines that became the building blocks for the lightweight cycle beauties of today.

The company kept growing and innovating. This led to a major milestone in cycle history, the introduction of the 50-cc Super Cub in the later 1950s (also called the Honda 50). It was the first motorcycle specifically designed for the general public—and it was a small cycle. It seems safe to say you wouldn't be reading this book now if the Super Cub hadn't come along when it did. Before that, motorcycles were considered specialty items intended for a handful of individuals who wanted to tempt fate by riding dangerous routes at high speeds or performing difficult stunts. But Honda and his engineers felt that millions of former nonriders would flock to a low price, easy-to-ride two-wheeler. The massive response to the introduction of the Super Cub in Japan on August 1, 1958, proved their point.

In the early 1960s, Honda began thinking of the United States market. With the slogan "You meet the nicest people on a Honda" and a campaign pointing out that almost anyone could quickly become adept at riding, the company drew the attention of many Americans in the mid-sixties. (Though the major mass market emphasis was on a 50-cc model, the Honda lightweight-line introduced to buyers in the United States included several more powerful bikes using 90-cc engines.) It took a little while for the idea to catch on, but by the late 1960s Honda lightweight models alone were finding their way into American homes at the rate of a half million a year.

By the mid-1970s, the Honda lightweight cycle family included a range of designs with a variety of power options. In 1971-72, the original bellwether 50-cc C-100 model was replaced by a more powerful (though still lightweight and simple to operate) vehicle that used a 70-cc engine. The new engine, like the original 50-cc type, is a single cylinder, of four-stroke design, but with a piston displacement of 70 cc, plus refinements in the overall engine design. The new powerplant provides about 4.9 horsepower for street use compared to only about 3 horsepower in the earlier model. Its popularity has matched that of its predecessor with new riders. Meanwhile, many people who learned to love motor-

There's no sex discrimination on small cycles. In increasing numbers, girls like this one are demonstrating expert riding style.

cycling on the Super Cub series were moving up to more versatile higher performance lightweights in the 90-, 100- and 125-cc categories.

The Honda experience in Japan and the United States wasn't lost on other cycle makers. By the end of the 1960s, new designs in all lightweight ranges were rolling off production lines in Japan and Europe. Contenders from Japan came from such major firms as Kawasaki, Suzuki and Yamaha. Excellently performing bikes in the 125-cc and under range also began arriving from such European producers as Benelli, Bultaco, Fox, Husqvarna and Jawa. One of the few remaining cycle builders in the United States, Harley-Davidson, also joined the parade. An old-line firm primarily famous for rugged, very powerful cycles in the large bike classifications, Harley-Davidson started looking to the general market with several 125-cc designs in the 1960s. At the start of the seventies, it turned out smaller models, such as its "Shortster," powered by a 65-cc two-stroke engine with integral three-speed transmission.

In 1969 several companies in the United States and Japan almost simultaneously inaugurated the minibike idea. The minibike derived from the earlier, usually homemade bicycles where the power was gained by installing lawn mower motors on conventional bikes. Those designs were very inefficient and also were generally agreed to be unsafe. Motorcycle engineers finally began to realize the possible advantages of designing simple little cycles that would incorporate the features of a good cycle. These could be offered for much lower costs than regular designs, even the lightweights pioneered by Honda, and promised to permit many more people to sample the joys of cycling. Engineering experts devised special motorcycle frames for the small engines and, before long, minibikes were available throughout the world.

In nation after nation, cycling has become tremendously popular and has sparked introduction of a bewildering array of powered two-wheelers. With motorcycle builders continuing to provide new selections to cover every imaginable kind of riding, a critical problem facing new enthusiasts is deciding which bike to buy. If you consider minibikes alone, a typical buyers' guide issue of a motorcycle magazine shows dozens of different designs from various manufacturers. Adding in small cycles for such categories as street cycles, off-road bikes, combination on-off road bikes and dirt racers, the possible spectrum goes well over 100 different models. Even if you're an experienced motorcyclist, you

24

find the array of performance figures, dimensions (and conflicting manufacturers' claims) so vast that it's difficult to decide what design best fits your present riding needs.

It's nice, of course, to have such an impressive range of options. It means, if you can sort things out, that there should be a machine on the market that almost perfectly matches your requirements. But to do this you have to find ways of somehow making the right choice before you spend hundreds of dollars on a wrong number.

There are several steps that can help narrow the field. You can study test-ride reports. You'll find these in leading cycle publications, such as *Cycle Magazine, Cycle Guide, Mini-Bike Guide* and *Motor Cycle World.* Several of these publish annual catalog issues that present excellent roundups of the new motorcycle market.

While this helps channel the possibilities, you'll find it generally still leaves too many alternatives for an easy choice. You can cut down your list further by discussing cycle capabilities with a friend or two who have ridden various small-cycle models. By far the best approach, however, is to go to dealer showrooms to inspect closely various designs and follow with test rides of models that interest you.

A test ride is really the only meaningful way for you to judge cycle quality. This means you need a certain amount of background before making a commitment. For one, of course, you have to be able to ride. You also have to find out first what's involved in small cycles—how they work, the differences among major classifications, and what the experts recommend as the best ways to operate a modern powered two-wheeler.

2
BIG BIKE, LITTLE BIKE

There is no such thing as a minibike! That, at least, is what you'll find if you compare most minibike models to "official" definitions. You'll learn that the same holds true in many cases if you try to classify some bikes as "big" or "little."

For years bike fans and some dealers have urged the motorcycle industry to pinpoint the basic features of its classes. Somewhat reluctantly, the cycle-building fraternity has tried to do this for minibikes, but the results have been far from spectacular. For instance, here is the 1971 pronouncement by the Motorcycle Industry Council "defining" a minibike:

"All or any of the following characteristics on a two-wheeled vehicle, except a scooter, would classify the vehicle as a minibike: (1) less than a 10-inch wheel diameter; (2) less than a 40-inch wheelbase; (3) less than a 45-cc engine; (4) less than a 25-inch seat height, measured at the lowest point of the seat cushion without a rider."

A glance at any current manufacturer's catalog or the lists in buyers' guide issues of cycle magazines should convince you that practically no model called a minibike meets all these criteria. A high percentage does not meet any of them. Almost every well-designed minibike of today uses at least a 50-cc engine and many have powerplants with double and triple that displacement. Many have higher seats and some have wheels with considerably greater tire diameters. Some experts in the mid-1970s suggested using a maximum tire diameter of 16 inches, combined with specifying "solid wheels" (that is, wheels having a metal-type hub rather than open-wire construction) to define the class. Hardly had the proposal been voiced than minibikes began appearing with wheels over 16 inches and even sporting wire hubs rather than solid wheels on some 10-inch diameter models.

We might try another approach, using a more general-size relationship between major classes. We might say a big bike is a strong, powerful machine that can run faster, go farther, and carry more "payload" weight; a lightweight is somewhat less powerful and not as rugged; a minibike is smallest of all—more a plaything than a bike. Something like Papa Bear, Mama Bear, and Baby Bear. But it cannot be made that simple. Recent advances in technology and bike engineering make it possible to get performance once restricted to fairly large machines from much smaller ones. Get out your company catalogs again and you'll see that what is called a minibike by one company may be classed as a small cycle by another. Viewing it another way, the specifications given for some models defined as minibikes are similar to what would be expected for a lightweight street or trail model.

A similar situation exists between lightweight models and larger bikes. You won't have much problem telling the really big bikes from the lightweights. (For one thing, the big bikes have equally big prices.) But when you try to separate the lightweight from the medium, it's another story. Taking displacement as a rough guide, some authorities draw the line for lightweight or small bikes at 100 cc, some at 125, some as high as 175-200 cc.

Most experts generally consider the range for medium bikes to extend from whatever lower limit they choose up to about 599 cc. The large models are then rated from 600 cc up. The grouping might be based on weight or speed rather than engine displacement, particularly since there once was a very close relationship between all these factors. For instance, it once was an accepted rule of thumb that a 100-cc model weighed about 200 pounds and could hit 60 MPH, a 250 cc was about 300 pounds with 100 MPH the top speed, and so on. But, as discussed, recent improvements in engine systems and structural materials let designers achieve the same speed and overall performance for much less bike weight.

However, some criterion is necessary. For this reason, we will arbitrarily select 125-cc displacement as the upper limit for lightweight, small cycles.

One answer to this confusing situation would be for industry members to get together and agree on standards, then design models to fit in neat categories. The problem is that every manufacturer thinks any standards should use his specifications as the point of reference. Apart from that, some bike makers would rather leave things as they are because it makes it harder for the buyer to see clearly that a competitor's model may be better.

In self-defense, then, you should try to learn as much about how bikes work as possible. At the very least you should try to understand the basic principles of cycle operation. With this as a starting point, you can move on to sort out what the numbers for speeds, gear ratios, and other performance factors mean in terms of what you really want to do on a bike.

When it comes to basic principles, at least you're on firm ground, because no matter what the size, engine output, gearing and the like, the operating ground rules essentially are the same for all bikes. Obviously motorcycles are two-wheelers, although a motorcycle with a sidecar—a three-wheeler—is also accepted as a motorcycle. In this case, however, the operating portion is still really a two-wheeler.

The bike's wheels are connected to the main frame by front and rear fork assemblies. On just about all modern motorcycles the forks are fitted with suspension systems, such as springs or hydraulic cylinders, to absorb energy from bumps or other shocks. To let you steer the bike, the handlebars attach to the front fork.

In addition to the seat, the other main items are the power delivery system and the controls. The power system comprises the engine, fuel and oil system, the transmission and the drive system. The drive system on all bikes of interest in this book makes use of chains just like your bicycle does. In bigger bikes, though, you can find models in which the rear wheel is turned by rotating linkages that work like the drive system of an automobile. Besides the all-important brakes, the controls include a starter system, throttle, clutch lever and a gear-change system.

Naturally the heart of the machine is the powerplant, the internal combustion engine. The word "internal" denotes the fact that burning of the fuel-air mixture takes place inside the basic engine rather than outside it. Once the engine is started, it keeps running by means of a series of explosions of fuel and air inside housings known as cylinders. These explosions cause a piston (or pistons) to move up and down in the housings. The piston has a rod from its lower surface that connects to a crankshaft so that the up-and-down motion of the piston is changed into a rotating movement of the crankshaft. The crankshaft's rotation, in turn, makes a front sprocket revolve. This makes the chain drive turn the rear sprocket, which is attached to the rear wheel. It is the rotating action of the rear wheel, of course, that propels the bike ahead.

The concept, as you can see, is simple and straightforward. Of course, if you were an engineer making this process work efficiently in a modern motorcycle, it would be another matter. You would have to make hundreds of related decisions to reach your goal. For instance, an engine may be a two-stroke or four-stroke design: have one, two or more cylinders: use any of a variety of ways of getting the right mixture of fuel and air into the combustion chamber, and so forth. The cycle designer must figure out the best way to get the engine started and, once started, to have the right components so that the engine will run as smoothly as possible. Then the engineer has to work out the best way to get the power produced by the engine to the rear sprocket so the bike will do what it's supposed to do—speed up or slow down without stalling, accelerate fast enough in response to your control changes, and so on. This calls for choosing a certain number of gears with the proper gear ratios in the transmission system to accomplish the desired operating performance.

And there are plenty of other things. The action of the throttle in increasing or decreasing the amount of fuel mixture delivered to the engine must be coordinated with the workings of the other assemblies. The exhaust system must carry off the burned gases efficiently and be properly muffled to keep noise to reasonable levels. For off-road designs it needs spark arresters to prevent the exhaust from starting fires. The frame must distribute the loads so that no damage results to the cycle parts under any expected operating conditions. And the brakes must stop the bike effectively and reliably.

For compactness the motorcycle designer may make one system serve more than one role as is sometimes done with the flywheel. The flywheel is a relatively heavy metal wheel you'll find attached to the crankshaft. Its

Both of these Hondas are powered by 50cc engines, but there is a world of difference between the design of the solid tire minibike, QA-50 K3 above, and the MR-50 K1 below, which amounts to a small cycle.

main job is to compensate for sudden changes in piston forces that might cause the engine to run roughly. It's based on one of the basic laws of motion discovered by Sir Isaac Newton: a body at rest tends to remain at rest, and a body in motion tends to remain in motion unless either is operated on by an external force.

You might ask why piston forces vary. The reason is that the explosions of the fuel-air mixture are never exactly the same. Sometimes they exert more force on the piston than the engine needs to drive the load. When this happens, an uncontrolled engine would rapidly increase its speed. The inertia, or resistance to change, of the flywheel opposes such a speedup by absorbing the excess energy from the piston. On the other hand, when the cylinder forces are smaller than needed, which could make the engine slow down abruptly, the flywheel's inertia acts in the opposite way and adds energy to keep up the speed. The flywheel, as in the automobile and other systems using an internal combustion engine, ensures that the output of the crankshaft is smooth and constant.

In some motorcycle engines—but not all—the continuous revolution of the flywheel is put to another use: generation of the electric spark needed for fuel-air ignition in the combustion chamber. It's accomplished by installing a series of small magnets on the flywheel. (An example of this is the ignition system for Honda's small cycles, such as the QA50, Z50A and CT70).

The magnets, as they revolve, go past a coil of wire. The wire, in turn, is connected by a wire cable to the top end of a spark plug. The plug, which fits into the cylinder head, houses an electrically conductive metal wire, such as copper or tungsten, with a small bare section extending into the combustion chamber. The bare section, called the spark plug point, amounts to a metal loop with a tiny gap cut in it. As the magnets rotate around the coil, an electric charge is induced in them. At intervals, the electricity from the coil flows through the cable into the spark plug. To complete the circuit, the electric current jumps the small gap in the plug, causing a spark. (The size of the gap, which is important for the engine to work right, is on the order of 0.02-0.03 inch.) The spark ignites the explosion that drives the piston down. As you might expect, the engine design coordinates the timing of the spark with other actions, such as the introduction of fresh fuel-air mixture and the upward piston movement just before the spark occurs.

The combination of magnets and an electric coil is called a magneto. The flywheel installation is handy, but it isn't always the best approach, so don't be surprised to find the motorcycle you're interested in has a different setup. The magneto may be a completely separate unit or the ignition system may use a coil device in which electricity is built up in the coils alone without having a magneto. As you often find in technology, the various methods have advantages and disadvantages whose merits are often argued by motorcycle engineers.

As in any internal combusion engine, delivering the right mixture of fuel and air to the cylinders is of vital concern. The typical engine runs on regular gasoline, so you can roll up to the gas pump at any station and fill 'er up. Bike racers may use more powerful substances, but we're concerned here with minibikes, not minibombs. The fuel provides the material to be burned while the air supplies the oxygen needed to support combustion. For you to have a good-running bike, the correct amounts of fuel and air must be combined each time. For instance, if too much fuel is sent to the engine on each cycle, flooding may take place. If this happens, the engine won't start or, if running, may stall out.

The place where the fuel and air are mixed before entering the combustion chamber is the carburetor. It has an opening through which fuel comes in from the gas tank. The basic principle on which the device operates is called the "Venturi effect," named after the scientist who discovered it. A Venturi consists of a tube or pipe with a restriction in it. The restriction affects the speed and pressure of gas flowing through the tube. Once the gas (for our system, air) is past the restriction it is moving faster then when it came into it. To balance its properties, the pressure of the gas goes down. In the carburetor the lower pressure creates a suction effect that draws in a certain amount of fuel that has been turned into a fine spray of small droplets in the fuel system. If the size of the restriction is changed, the amount of air flowing through the tube is changed and, in turn, the amount of fuel-air mixture reaching the engine.

The operation of the carburetor is controlled by the throttle. On your cycle you'll find the throttle control located on the right handlebar. You open or close it by a twisting action of your right hand. When you twist the throttle grip, it moves a cable that operates the carburetor valves that meter the amount of air and fuel going into the cylinders. When you turn the throttle to reduce fuel and air flow, you lower the forces generated in the cylinders by the explosions and the bike slows down. If you turn the throttle the other way, the reverse takes place and the speed goes up. If you completely close the throttle, the engine doesn't shut down but instead goes to the idling mode. During idling, the carburetor is designed to have a special setting so that just enough fuel-air mixture passes through it to keep the engine running.

As you might expect, most minibikes and some of the smaller lightweight bikes have simpler carburetors than larger ones. For instance, all of Honda's minibikes presently use a carburetor called a "mechanical type variable venturi," while the lightweight models offer a more sophisticated "dash pot" design. You can see the differences between the two by looking at the diagrams.

In the minibike system, motion of the throttle cable changes the pressure on a spring that moves a slide-control valve in or out to control the air flow. As you can see, in both variable venturi and dash pot units, a needle valve is attached to the slide that moves with it to meter the amount of fuel. The needle valve compensates for the fact that the fuel flow into the carburetor doesn't have a straight line relation to the air-flow rate through the venturi. Without an adjusting device, the amount of gasoline vapor sent into the carburetor would go up faster than the increase of air going through the venturi.

You'll find the dash pot unit on most Honda bikes other than minis. Here, your movement of the throttle opens or closes a butterfly valve on the engine side of the carburetor. Changing the butterfly's position changes the pressure of the incoming air behind it. This pressure acts against the slide to move it up or down. When the slide moves, so does the attached needle value that controls fuel flow. As you can see, the slide is operated by air pressure rather than the direct spring-loaded method of the minibike system. To keep the slide from moving suddenly with rapid air-pressure changes there is an oil reservoir, called a dash pot. The oil smooths out the slide's movement by interacting with a small damping piston. You can see this little piston in the sketch just above the needle value attachment point.

Now let's see what is done with the power provided by fuel explosions. The output of the moving piston (or pistons) is transferred to the crankshaft, which converts it to rotating motion. We know that the number of revolutions of the crankshaft must increase to make the bike go faster and decrease for it to slow down. But before either of these comes into play, the bike obviously must be moving. Before it can get going, the engine must build up enough power to overcome inertia and the friction between wheels and ground. Some method is needed to avoid damage to the engine when the revolutions per minute (RPM) are too low to start the bike moving or to go from one speed level to another. The device used for this is called the clutch. It disconnects the powerplant from the drive system when the engine is building up or slowing down its rotating action to the proper levels for good performance.

In its simplest form, the clutch consists of two plates or disks, one on the output end of the crankshaft and one on the input end of the transmission. When the clutch control is released, the two mesh so that the rotation of the engine moves through into the gearbox. You operate the clutch control from a hand-squeezed lever attached to the left handlebar. When you actuate it, the two plates are separated and the engine is freed from the load.

The amount of energy the engine must send to the driving wheel varies with road conditions and with your desires in terms of cruise speed. To do this, you need some way of stepping the engine RPM up and down in relation to the rotating speed of the rear wheel. Though there are other ways of doing it, just about all present day motorcycles control bike speed through a series of gears.

The gears, located in the transmission box, consist of one set on a shaft fastened to the crankshaft side and a second set on a shaft fastened to the forward sprocket of the drive chain system. When you shift gears, you bring different combinations of gears together at a time, one on each shaft. These combinations are chosen so that one gear will have more teeth or less teeth than its partner, so that for a certain number of revolutions of one gear the other will turn through either a greater or lesser number of revolutions. For example, if the engine-side gear is turning at 4,000 RPM and, for each turn of that gear, the sprocket-side gear turns 1.25 times, the sprocket will rotate at 5,000 RPM.

At one time almost every motorcycle used three gears. With the introduction of more powerful engines and increasing performance demands, however, engineers found it advantageous to add gears. Today you'll find many bike models providing four, five, up to eight gears or more. But remember that extra gears are not necessarily an indication of a better bike. Engineers often have to add gears to make one bike do two different jobs or, in some cases, to compensate for the bike's having a poor powerband.

The word *powerband* refers to the range between the low end operating RPM of the engine to the highest rate at which it is considered safe for it to run. When the engine is started, as noted earlier, it must work up to the proper number of revolutions to handle the load. The load consists of the weight of the bike, the rider, and any equipment being taken along. Let's say the initial operating rate is 4,000 RPM. If the top speed the engine is designed to achieve is 7,500 RPM, then the powerband is 3,500 RPM. If the numbers are 3,000 and 5,500, the powerband is 2,500, and so on.

If you're planning to get a minibike, this review of powerbands isn't of great interest. Most minibikes aren't intended for very high speed or long range riding and so don't call for transmission of a lot of power to the rear sprocket. But it is an important consideration if you want a lightweight cycle for extensive use. In choosing such a bike, it generally holds true that for good acceleration performance, the wider the powerband, the better.

As far as minibike transmissions are concerned, a lot of them use only one or two gears. Many models, such as Honda's minis, don't use manual gear shifting at all, but have automatic transmissions. The automatic transmission makes it a lot easier if you're a beginner. You don't have to worry about the clutch lever. All you have to do is press or raise a foot pedal to go from one gear to the next. Someday the automatic transmission may become almost universal, as it has in the automobile. For the present, however, you should master the manual shift, because you'll need that ability when you move from a mini to a more powerful model.

As important as getting a cycle going is to have an efficient way of slowing it down and stopping. Just about all models, from minis up, have brakes on both front and rear wheels. The braking methods are similar to those used on automobiles: either the use of curved friction surfaces that clamp around a rotating section on the wheel axle assembly when the brake control is depressed, or the use of small disks that press on both sides of a plate attached to the axle. The trend in recent years has been toward disk brakes because these tend to be simpler and more effective than most brake-shoe systems.

The front brakes are controlled by a lever attached to the right handlebar. You control the rear brake with a foot pedal. This foot pedal may be on either side of the bike, depending on the model. If you're familiar with automobile operation you might assume that you get the main braking action from the rear brake. Not on a motorcycle, however! The front hand brake gives you something like three times the braking effect of the rear one.

The brief earlier decription of how the engine fits into the operation of the bike emphasizes the engine's role as the heart of the motorcycle. So, if you want to rate as a cycle buff, you should understand the main types of engines used on minibikes and lightweights and how they work.

The two broad groupings into which all these engines fall are two-stroke and four-stroke. (These engine classes are also referred to as two-cycle and four-cycle.) The words refer to the number of times the piston goes up and down for each fuel-air explosion, each movement being a stroke or cycle. In a two-stroke design the piston moves down once and then back up. At the top of the upward stroke the spark plug is energized to ignite the mixture. The explosion, or power stroke, begins only when the piston approaches top position the first time. The four-stroke requires movable intakes and exhaust valves and associated equipment; the two-stroke does not.

Built into the metal housing of a two-stroke engine are the passages through which the fuel mixture enters the cylinder and burned gases are exhausted. The passage openings, called ports, are exposed in proper order by the movement of the piston assembly. In a typical two-stroke design, as the piston moves upward, its bottom surface uncovers an intake port. At the same time its upper surface closes an opening called a transfer port. The lower entrance to the transfer port passageway is roughly opposite the intake port at the base of the cylinder housing. The upper opening is placed about halfway up the cylinder wall. The upward action of the piston creates a vacuum that causes a supply of fuel mixture to come into the crankcase through the intake port and move toward the transfer port. Meanwhile, there already is a charge of fuel and air in the top part of the cylinder that is being compressed into a smaller and smaller volume by the piston.

When the piston is at its highest point the spark plug explodes the fuel mixture, sending the piston down on the second, or power stroke. As it

39

This Yamaha RS 100B small street bike has a maximum speed of 68 mph. The single cylinder engine has a displacement of 97cc and provides a maximum torque of 7.0 feet per pound at 7,000 RPM.

moves down its top (or crown) first uncovers the exhaust port, then the transfer port. The incoming supply of fresh fuel mixture, given a "shove" by the bottom of the piston, sweeps through the transfer port up into the top of the cylinder. Its movement helps push the burned gases out the exhaust port. After the piston reaches the bottom of the power stroke it starts up again to repeat the process.

A variation of the two-stroke method, called the rotary value two-stroke cycle, is favored by a number of cycle manufacturers. In this system, intake of the fuel mixture from the carburetor is controlled by a metal disk attached to the crankshaft instead of by the piston surface. A small section of the disk is cut away so that it opens the passage from the carburetor at the proper time in the cycle. Companies using this design in minibikes and small cycles include Kawasaki and Yamaha.

The four-stroke engine has no ports in its cylinder walls. Instead, intake and exhaust of the fuel mixture are handled by two small valves, usually located in the cylinder head in modern engines. These are opened and closed at the correct moments in the cycle by small, specially shaped parts called cams. The cams are fastened to a rotating arm called a camshaft. Some engine designs have the camshaft located in the crankcase, but the majority of present day four-stroke designs have it installed above the cylinder head. The latter are called overhead cam engines. The system can be designed so one cam operates both valves; you'd call this a single overhead cam system (SOHC). Or there can be two cams, one for each valve, in the double overhead cam system (DOHC). You'll find minibikes and lightweights almost always using the SOHC method with DOHC's applied on medium to large models.

The four-stroke method, the same basic principle used in almost all automobile engines, begins with the intake stroke. As the piston moves down, the camshaft opens the intake valve and the low pressure region created by the piston's motion sucks in a charge of fuel and air from the carburetor. When the piston reaches the bottom point in its travel, the cam closes the intake valve. As rotation of the crankshaft to which the piston is connected moves the piston upward, both valves are closed and the top of the piston compresses the fuel-air mixture.

(This is a good time to take a moment to define a term you'll hear a lot when engine performance is discussed: the compression ratio. This is the ratio of the volume in the cylinder when the piston is at its lowest position and the final volume into which the fuel mixture is squeezed.)

Just before the piston completes the second, or compression stroke, a surge of electricity passes through the spark plug initiating the third, or power, stroke. The expanding gases push the piston down, causing the crankshaft to rotate. At the end of the power stroke the camshaft opens the exhaust valve. On the forth movement, the exhaust stroke, the piston moves up, pushing the burned gases out into the exhaust system. At the top of this stroke, the exhaust valve closes, the intake valve opens, and the process repeats itself.

The performance of a two- or four-stroke engine can be varied in many ways. Increasing the compression ratio can increase power. One very effective method of increasing the power output is to increase the number of power strokes, and thus the number of crankshaft revolutions, in a given period of time. Great progress has been made in both engine types in recent years by doing this. For example, engines of 50- and 100-cc displacement are now widely used that have ratings as high as 12,000 RPM and more.

In general, motorcycle engineers stay with three possible cylinder groupings: single; twin or four cylinder with the multicylinder models having the cylinders either parallel and vertical, horizontally opposed or in a ''V'' arrangement. There are pros and cons for each of these, which you can find in engineering books on motorcycle design. For lightweight bikes, though, you don't have to worry about that. Almost every model uses a single cylinder engine because of the great simplicity it offers. In any event, most designers aren't concerned with numbers of cylinders, but rather with the relative merits of a two-stroke and four-stroke engine.

The two-stroke can operate without a separate oil pump, a feature can be much lighter, simpler, and less expensive than a four-stroke. Especially because of low cost, the two-stroke reigned supreme for many years in the motorcycle field. But the engine also has disadvantages. It tends to shake and vibrate more than a four-stroke, and deposits of carbon and other impurities can build up rapidly on its port surfaces. This can make the two-stroke harder to start than a four-stroke and sometimes can require an overhaul sooner than its competitor.

The two-stroke can operate without a separate oil pump, a feature which may be considered either good or bad. Oil still must be provided to prevent damage to moving parts. For a long time cyclists had to mix oil and gasoline in correct proportions while filling a two-stroke fuel tank.

This disadvantage has been minimized in recent years thanks to the introduction of special oil-injection systems. Examples are the Suzuki Crankshaft Cylinder Injection System and Yamaha's Autolube. The engine still needs a mixture of oil and gas to run right, but the new systems automatically add the right amount of oil from small oil reservoirs.

On the other hand, the four-stroke is more expensive than the two-stroke and theoretically has more that can go wrong because of the added systems it needs. However, it offers very smooth, almost foolproof operation if properly designed. It also runs cooler than the two-stroke and theoretically has more that can go wrong because of the every four piston movements instead of every other movement. The four-stroke features smoother operation over a greater range of speeds than the two-stroke and also is less likely to stall out during idling. A separate pump and delivery system for lubrication is used since the four-stroke doesn't use oil in the fuel.

For a long time many cycle experts looked down on the four-stroke. They thought it was too complicated for the average rider to maintain properly and that its higher price would drive away prospective buyers. Honda engineers disagreed. The company gambled it could come up with a highly reliable four-stroke that would give excellent service without demanding unreasonable technical skills of the bike owner. You can see the result today in many dealer showrooms and on the road. The four-stroke is very popular indeed. Honda has few two-strokes in its line and has won much applause for the performance of its four-stroke systems. Even its minibikes are all four-stroke powered.

The two-stroke is far from a has-been. Suzuki, Yamaha, and European manufacturers have steadily met the four-stroke challenge with improvements in design and performance far beyond what some observers thought possible a few years back. For some applications, such as trail bikes or motorcycle racing, the simplicity and reliability of a good two-stroke engine give it a clear edge over most four-stroke candidates.

Though rotary Wankels are beginning to be applied in some big bikes, it seems certain that the conventional two- and four-stroke engines will be used in new motorcycles for a long time to come. If you learn the correct riding techniques and learn good maintenance procedures, a cycle powered by either type of engine will give you many hours of practical use and enjoyment.

3

RIDE, RIDE, RIDE

You have the "two-wheel" itch. You've looked at catalogs and visited showrooms to gaze at some of those shiny new lightweights. Perhaps you've envied the ease with which your friends hop into the saddle and pilot their own mounts around the neighborhood. You'd like to try it yourself, but you naturally don't want to smash up someone else's equipment and your friends may not be overly eager for that either. For that matter, if you get your own bike, there's not much percentage in turning it into a candidate for the junkman by foolish mistakes.

Luckily you can easily avoid all these pitfalls. You can get aid from expert instructors at little or no cost by going to one of the many riding clinics set up by bike makers and other organizations. You can find the details of when and where by asking. Ask a member of a cycle club. Ask any motorcycle dealer. Ask at the YMCA or YWCA. A majority of these courses are free, and, while it's nice to learn on your own bike, many organizations provide you with two-wheelers if you don't have your own yet.

When you enroll in one of these training programs, you'll find the bikes they use are well-designed minis and lightweights. These types have been widely adopted by instructors because they are uncomplicated and inexpensive, factors just as important for later riding pleasure as for the learning experience. But note the emphasis on "well-designed" bikes. Skilled cycle instructors avoid small cycles that essentially are limited playthings, knowing they are of little value in helping you develop good riding habits. You can put this fact to good use in another way. Before you buy a bike, you might want to get some pointers from instructors on what to look for when choosing one. (Of course, we'll try to give you some hints on the matter in the following chapters as well). For recommendations on specific makes, it's wise to search out people not involved with specific bike manufacturers for impartial estimates. This is not meant to downgrade cycle builders' training efforts; some of the most thorough, best organized courses are the free ones offered by Honda, Yamaha, Suzuki, and the like.

There's obviously no substitute for the real thing. You have to master operation of a cycle by riding it. That's what you want to do anyway. But reading literature on the fine points before, during or after a riding course can help. You can find a growing list of books dealing with the subject. Some can be found in local libraries or you can contact cycle companies, dealers or the Motorcycle Industry Council, 1001 Connecticut Avenue, N.W., Washington, D.C. 20036. Reading these pages and reviewing some riding basics may be worthwhile even if you aren't a beginner. Finding out what experts consider the right approach to cycle operation may point the way to much more relaxed riding. It's never too late to unlearn a bad habit and substitute a good one.

Swift movement and the promise of carefree moments may have attracted you to cycling, but to realize these goals, patience is a prime virtue. As one instructor points out, "You have to want to take the time and effort needed to get all the steps in operating a motorcycle down pat. You can't get impatient and start taking off every which way over all kinds of roads and trails as soon as you know how to get the bike going. And you always have to have respect for the vehicle itself. You have to run it right and do all the many little things that must be done constantly to ensure your bike is in the best condition."

If you're a beginner, the first step is familiarization. Start with the owner's manual. Read it through a time or two, then compare it to the actual motorcycle to see where the controls are placed and to find the locations of parts that need checking. The manual should come with the bike if you've bought a new one. If you're using one supplied by a training school and the manual is missing, ask a dealer for one or write the manufacturer.

Familiarization is the first step in learning to ride. Here an instructor explains the proper way to operate a minibike's hand control to a beginner.

Obviously, one of the priorities is to study the controls. It would be nice if all the bike models had controls in exactly the same positions. Logically there's no reason why the industry shouldn't set standards on this, but no one wants to change production lines. So you have to look over every unfamiliar model to check out control locations. All bikes have the throttle control on the right handlebar and the front brake lever on the same side. In addition, all bikes with a manual transmission have the clutch lever attached to the left handlebar. We've already noted that some bikes, particularly in the minibike class, have automatic transmissions which don't require a clutch lever. At this writing, the majority of lightweights and larger models have manual transmissions.

The two controls you have to pay particular attention to are the gear-shift pedal and the rear brake. Depending on the model, these may be on either side of the bike. In general, you'll find all models produced by a particular manufacturer maintain common locations for these controls. Still, don't take anything for granted; always check it out. If you go from one make to a model from another firm, however, there's a good chance the positions will vary.

Your main concern with the brake pedal is to see which side it's on. But you should also see if it's in a slightly different position relative to the ground compared to what you're used to. That can affect the feel of the pedal. With the gear shift, you must not only know which side it's on, but also the shifting sequence. That isn't too crucial for many minibikes because there are only a few shift positions. But for higher performance small cycles with three, four, five or more gears, you should study the shifting procedure more closely.

Even with one or two gears, you must know if you depress the pedal with your toe to go from low to high gear or if you should raise it instead. When your bike has a number of gears, the lowest gear may be located below the neutral position, with the other gears above neutral. In that case you have to push the pedal all the way down to get it into first, then raise it past neutral for second, third or higher. You might find a model where the opposite holds true or the sequence might be varied in a completely different way.

Now that you've studied the diagrams and walked around the bike a number of times getting control positions straight in your mind, you're ready to get the feel of the bike. You're not going to scoot down the road

An instructor steadies the bike as a new rider gets the feel of her mount.

until you've put in a period of dry runs. There's an old saying: "A journey of a thousand miles starts with a single step." So there's something to remember about the first move you make toward a bike: mount it from the safe side. This means you get on from the curb side, away from traffic. It's a simple rule, but some people who ignore it end up heading for the doctor instead of the open road.

While an intructor or accomplished rider steadies the bike and schools you in proper methods, you sit in the saddle with the bike at rest and practice the right way to use your hands and feet. Part of this phase includes studying the fuel system components, such as the gas valve, gas tank cap valve, ignition and choke. With the ignition switch off and the bike resting on its support, you can begin some dry runs—that is, practicing how to start and run the bike without actually applying the power. You also must rehearse the starting procedure, which involves kicking the starting lever with one foot to get the engine going. (Some bikes have replaced the kick starter with an electric starting system. However, the majority retain the kick starter and, like the clutch, you should know how to use it.)

It's a good idea to use the dry run approach on any bike that's considerably different from the one you're used to riding. Experts know this. Cal Rayborn, before setting a new world's motorcycle speed record in the early 1970s, did not just straddle the new superpowered two-wheeler provided by Harley-Davidson and take off down the Bonneville Salt Flats. Like any beginner, he studied the bike carefully and then spent many hours practicing control methods, first with the engine off, later with it running but held in a form of treadmill operation.

While staying in place, you have to learn to position your feet properly on the foot pegs, which are located a little behind the foot-operated controls. The pegs act as a resting place for your feet when you're cruising and as pivot points on which to rotate your feet while working the pedals.

Only after spending a lot of time practicing the preceding steps are you ready to turn on the ignition key. Before doing this, though, it's a must that you have the proper clothing and accessories—unless, that is, you'd rather be numb and shivering instead of snug and warm when the cold winds blow or would prefer extra bumps and bruises. Assuming riding and not self-inflicted punishment is your aim, you need a strong, well-fitting helmet and goggles; a sweat shirt with long sleeves; good gloves; long, straight-cut pants; and heavy leather shoes or boots. This is the minimum for riding on local streets or in backyards. When the time comes for journeys to the backcountry, you'll want added protection, such as a leather or heavy vinyl jacket, and riding pants and high boots.

The second phase in a well-managed riding program is restricted riding. In this stage you gradually learn to run the bike from startup into first gear while the instructor, parent or friend holds the seat or frame to prevent a sudden "jackrabbit" start. Naturally you have to learn the proper balance to keep the bike upright. However, it's actually a simpler thing to master on a motorcycle than a bicycle because a well-designed cycle takes advantage of physical principles known as gyroscopic effects. These effects result in a condition of "auto-stability" once the engine gets the cycle up to a certain minimum speed of about 5 to 10 MPH.

Above that speed the bike wheels essentially become gyroscopes rotating around an invisible axis. The forces acting on the wheel under these conditions always tend to keep the wheel upright and self-balanced unless a very violent force is applied tending to force it over. Thus, if you relax once up to speed and keep your weight evenly distributed on the foot pegs, the bike basically does the rest.

Before going on to supervised riding you should first demonstrate good bike control under restricted conditions. Once you've done this, you're ready to "solo" over special practice courses set up in an empty parking lot, playground, or other open area. The routes are outlined by marking them with plastic bottles or hay bales.

In a typical program you might start out on a simple oval course, riding slowly in low gear at the outset, then carefully working up to cruise speed. The instructor will test your reflexes by unexpectedly signaling stops from time to time. After this the instructor may set up a figure-eight course on which you can practice left and right turns. Before graduating, you have to demonstrate skill and coordination over a curving course by weaving in and out of a long series of hay bales or obstacles. Then you're ready for off-road practice routes where bike operation over longer distances and increasingly more intricate layouts is performed, including demonstration of good braking technique.

The skills developed in this way are good for local riding on side streets, backyards, and simple circuits in motorcycle parks. Remember, they must be polished and repolished before any effort is made to go out in rugged terrain or on main streets in traffic. It can't be stressed too much that while most minibikes may be operated safely in moderately unprepared regions, such as dirt trails and small hills, they are not intended for extensive off-road use and should never be operated in traffic. Before you match wits with four-wheelers, you should have a cycle designed for use in those conditions.

Assuming you have the proper motorcycle for more demanding applications, you should not undertake them without having gained the "feel" of the bike so well as to become almost a part of the machine. The skilled cyclist has gone through the correct routine so often it has become second nature. You should be able to get the bike started and know intuitively the right times to shift, apply brakes, and the like, without even looking at the positions and motions of your hands and feet.

Part of this involves being able to sense that the bike's systems are running the way they should so you can catch possible problems before they become dangerous. You should put this understanding of mechanical properties into play before even getting onto your cycle. You do it in the walk-around inspection that should be performed before you go out on the road. A typical checklist for this is given by Honda as follows:

• On bike, check throttle operation. Check cable for free play and proper adjustment.

• Make sure handlebars are in riding position and knobs are tight. Be sure brake cables are not pinched.

• Check free play and adjustment of brakes.

• Check gas level.

• Check tire air pressure.

• Check all screws and bolts for tightness and adjust if needed.

• Check oil level in crankcase, adding oil if needed.

• Check air filter and clean if dirty.

• Make sure the drive chain is oiled and has the proper play. (Typically a half-inch play for minibikes; for most lightweight cycles in the Honda line, such as the CL 125, standard slack for the chain midway between the sprockets is supposed to be in the range between 0.4 and 0.8 inch.)

• Observe general cleanliness of bike. Wash if necessary.

The last point, often ignored by unknowing riders, is important. Dirt or

You have to keep close watch over your equipment to make sure it's always in good running order. Tires are an example. You should have the right tread designs for the kind of riding you intend to do and you should inspect them regularly for proper inflation, absence of flat spots, and to make sure they're not getting worn down too much.

other debris in the bike can get into some of the operating parts and degrade performance. In addition, the buildup of dirt and grime on the metal fins that are built into the cylinder housings can be dangerous to engine life. Except for a few of the bigger cycles, almost all bikes are air cooled. The heat from the engine is dumped into the air by the external engine surfaces. You can see the engine fins have an in-and-out design. The purpose is to present the maximum metal surface to the air because the larger this area, the more heat that can be dissipated. If the fins are choked with dirt, less heat escapes from the cylinder and thus the engine will run hotter. In extreme cases—for example, where large amounts of mud get into the fin openings during off-trail riding—the heat could literally melt the piston.

Once the preliminary check is over, you're ready for the relatively easy moves needed to get underway. Straddling the cycle with both feet planted on the ground, turn the ignition key to on. (At rest, you should be able to reach the ground with both feet while seated on the saddle. If you can't do this, the seat is too high.) The gear shift should be in neutral. Keeping the kickstand down for better balance, fold out the kick starter, disengage the clutch by squeezing the control lever, and twist the throttle control a third turn in the open direction. Then place your instep on the starter and push down firmly with a locked knee, repeating this if necessary until the engine is running. Then fold both starter and stand back in.

Keep the gear in neutral while the engine is idling. After the engine has warmed up, pull in the clutch lever with your left-hand fingers, then move the gear pedal with your toes in the proper direction for first gear. Once in gear, slowly release the clutch lever and gradually twist the throttle grip inward with your right-hand fingers. Good coordination of these moves is a must for a smooth start and, later, for proper gear shifting.

Now you're on your way. When the motorcycle is going fast enough for the next gear (which is indicated on most general-use models by a series of red lines on the RPM gage), close the throttle, pull in the clutch lever, and raise or depress the gear pedal to the next gear position. In most cases, the shift from first to second gear is done at about 10 MPH. The sequence is repeated progressively as you move to each higher gear.

For slowing down or stopping, the above sequence is reversed, except that an added factor is involved, application of the brakes. The order of doing this is as follows: You twist down the hand throttle, smoothly depress the rear-brake foot pedal, squeeze the front-brake lever with your right-hand fingers and pull the clutch lever in with your left-hand fingers as you shift the gear to a lower setting.

A crucial "must" in all this is to follow these required moves in the same order each time. For instance, if you try to move the gear pedal before you depress the clutch lever, at best the engine may stall out, and at worst you might cause severe damage to the transmission. In normal riding, you actuate the rear brake a little before the front one because the front provides much more powerful braking action. A good balance of front and rear braking is important for effective slowing or stopping. In most situations if you apply the front brake first, you might find yourself flying through the air (but not like a bird) over the handlebars. On the other hand, using the rear brake alone could result in too slow a stop, which might bring such goodies as running a red light or ramming an obstacle ahead of your bike.

With constant practice you'll learn to sense automatically just how much braking action is needed from each control. Of course, experience teaches you when the normal sequence must be changed. One case where the rear brake should be used alone is at very slow speeds when you find it difficult to keep the front wheel lined up straight with the rear one. Actually, though, if you find yourself trying to maneuver your bike at very low speeds, you haven't mastered the correct technique. If the bike is slowed to only a few miles an hour without coming to a full stop, you haven't applied the brakes firmly enough.

As soon as the bike comes to a stop, you should put your gear foot down to the ground to balance it, momentarily keeping your other foot on the brake pedal. Then lower your brake foot and use your gear foot to shift into neutral. During this operation, you must keep both the front brake and clutch levers pulled in firmly. Once in neutral, you can release both, keeping both feet planted on the ground to keep the bike stationary.

If you're used to driving an automobile, you know that when you're stopped for a light or stop sign, the car remains in gear and is held in place by the brake pedal. This might make you feel the same thing should be done on a motorcycle. Instead of shifting into neutral, you might keep the transmission in low gear, planning on a fast start by releasing the clutch lever. However, as some experts point out, there are times when this could cause you and your bike to part company. This could occur if the clutch cable snapped with the bike in gear, which could cause the bike to shoot forward when you aren't expecting it. Shifting into neutral when stopped seems the wiser policy.

When you're cruising along under normal street conditions, you should keep your weight evenly distributed on the foot pegs and the seat. Hunching forward over the handlebars may look jazzy but, in most cases, it causes a poor weight distribution that increases the danger of the bike pitching up and over if the front wheel hits a wet spot. If you don't position yourself so your hindquarters are resting on the seat area, you'll be defeating the many hours of thinking that went into the bike's design.

One of the prime goals of a good cycle engineer is achieving just the right weight distribution to make the vehicle as stable as possible. The total weight of bike, rider and any equipment is concentrated at a single point called the center of gravity (CG). This weight must be transmitted to the ground at only two points, the front wheel and the rear one. If the CG is exactly in the middle of the bike-rider combination, the force on both wheels will be equal and the bike will be very stable. The CG can move to a certain extent backward or forward without greatly affecting the stability. But if it moves sharply forward toward the handlebars (or rearward, though rearward movement is harder to accomplish), much more weight is placed on the front wheel, and the bike becomes harder to control under most street conditions.

Good stability is important from side-to-side as well as fore-and-aft. If you have too much body weight on one footpeg, the bike naturally tends to lean that way. For straight and level riding, you'd then have to exert considerably more effort to keep the bike upright than if you were sitting squarely in place on saddle and pegs. Besides keeping your weight evenly on the pegs, you should also bring your knees close to the frame. There are times when you should stand up on the footpegs, examples being certain racing conditions or during some phases of trail riding. For the most part, though, the preceding example is the rule.

But all rules have exceptions. When road conditions change, there are times you'll have good reason to shift your weight around on the seat for improved control. An example is in operations on backcountry roads where obstacles are likely to crop up suddenly. Here you'd want to shift forward in the seat to put more force on the front wheel and thus overcome unexpected upward forces from stones, humps in the road and the like. On a wet road, you'd want to slide back in the seat to bear down on the rear wheel. Since the rear wheel is the one that transmits the drive force from the engine to the ground, it's important to keep it in good contact with the road surface to avoid slipping.

Because the tires provide the only two points for transmitting bike loads to the ground, you should pay close attention to them. If tires develop flat spots or become worn out, they can affect riding performance by shifting the ground contact points off-center. A worn tread also obviously affects tire traction and thus both driving efficiency and braking action. (Different kinds of tires are needed for different kinds of riding, which will be considered in more detail in the next chapter.) Tire pressure can vary the bike's operating performance and also can contribute to tire wear. Thus you should always make sure tire pressure is maintained at the level recommended by the manufacturer.

So far we've mainly discussed straight-line riding. But good cornering is very important. You must learn to slow down a little going into a turn, though not so much that the bike's balance between centrifugal and gravitational forces is disturbed. The major danger in cornering is trying to do it too fast. This is caused by the fact that forces tending to make tires lose adhesion to the road surface increase as speed goes up. Thus, at the limits of safe turning speed it takes only a little extra disturbing force to cause a tire to start sliding. Once this happens, the tire will lose its directional stability in all directions or, in other words, you'll lose control.

An extra disturbing force, in this case, might be the use of the brake. This is why experts will tell you the brake should not be used if you want to make a correct turn. Instead, you should achieve it by proper use of the throttle.

You use throttle control in cornering to accelerate your bike around a curve. You should come into the curve at a relatively slow speed, then gradually apply throttle until the turn is completed. The level of speed you should take through a curve will vary, depending on whether it is a right- or left-hand move. On a typical street or highway the shape of the roadway (it's sloped so rain will run off into the gutter) generally works with the rider on a right-hand turn. This lets you go in a little faster and accelerate to higher speeds than for a left-hand turn. For either turn, it's not a good idea to start too near the edge of the road. The guidelines are to go into a turn wide and come out close.

It's also important that you keep both feet up on the pegs and foot controls during a turn. Though racers may put down a foot on a high speed turn, it's dangerous and unnecessary in normal street or trail riding. When the racer drags a foot, he knows just how to do it without losing control of his mount. He also has special boots with steel plates on the bottom—otherwise he might find himself barefoot in a hurry. Even the expert racer will never use a foot when taking a curve on a normal, everyday cycling excursion.

Before you try off-road riding, it's important to have plenty of seasoning by developing good bike techniques on flat surfaces. Once the basics of starting, gear shifting, accelerating and decelerating are thoroughly mastered, you can turn your attention to the pleasures of sampling winding rural trails, unprepared forest routes, going up and down steep hills and the like.

For off-road riding, the points made earlier about being able to operate all controls by feel is, if anything, several times as vital as for street riding. On off-road routes you must continuously be looking ahead for bumps, potholes, logs, or even a small animal that might dart in front of you. The position for normal riding remains the same—knees hugging the gas tank, feet on the pegs with weight evenly balanced and toes pointed ahead. But in the backcountry you must be mentally alert and ready to change body position fast if an obstacle comes into view. If you detect a bump, you should stand up on the pegs as you go over it.

Going up hills you may also find it improves the balance to stand up on the pegs over some parts of the trail. When you're seated on an uphill grade, expert advice is that you lean forward to move the CG to a more balanced location. Conversely, on a downhill slope, you should lean back to put more weight on the rear wheel.

Braking requires close attention during hill riding. Going uphill the front brake is relied on to provide a lot of extra force to oppose the bike's tendency to slide back down if you come to a stop. But on a downhill run you must remember the front brake has to be applied very carefully. If you apply too much front brake all at once, your bike can go out of control or pitch over. Instead of using the front brake on a downhill slope, your best approach is to shift to second gear and allow the compression effects of the engine to provide braking power. You supplement this with a light use of your rear brake.

If you want to stop or if the engine stalls out, you should observe certain steps. For one thing, you should keep your feet on the pegs until the bike is completely stopped. Otherwise your foot might come down in a hole or rut or get snagged by a rock, which could lead to serious injury. The front-brake lever has to be pulled in sharply in the final phase of stopping, and you must school yourself always to dismount on the uphill side so that if the bikes topples over you won't end up underneath it.

In backcountry riding the password is "caution." The most experienced rider will take an unfamiliar trail slow and easy at first to make sure he sees all hazards. If you're a newcomer to trail riding, it's even more vital to go over a route before taking liberties with it to check out blind corners, potholes, or any large obstructions. This is important even if you went over the same trail only a week ago. Someone may have put up a cable in the interim, or rock slides or fallen trees may have closed off previously clear pathways. You also should scout a hill trail in rugged terrain to make sure it's possible to come back down safely once you get to the top.

One maneuver that comes in handy to clear trail obstacles is the wheelie. It looks like an exciting trick, and it is. It's not too difficult to master, but you should not approach it lightly. You accomplish it by pulling the handlebars up just before reaching the obstacle while almost simultaneously hitting the throttle, causing the cycle to jump over the obstacle. You have to practice until you know the distance you need between bike and obstacle before you pull up the front wheel. Naturally, you must also develop a feel for how much throttle to apply. The critical part of the maneuver is applying a lot of throttle to get a healthy push forward. If you use too little throttle, your bike can flip on its back. As with other cycling basics, learning wheelie technique calls for good instruction and a step-by-step progression from small or nondangerous objects (such as a plastic cone) to large obstacles.

4

SMALL BIKE PARADE

Let's say you're an accomplished rider or at least have made plans to learn to ride. It's time to get to the heart of the matter by examining the features of some actual two-wheelers.

Consider some of the bike requirements for different kinds of riding. There is no way, of course, we can make many absolute statements about the specific bike for you. The choice will vary with each individual and, most likely, the final decision will involve some kind of compromise. Luckily, as this review should indicate, the selection is so wide that if you choose carefully you won't have to compromise too much.

Just studying some of the detailed specifications for a variety of bikes can help you clarify the capabilities of modern cycles. The bikes reviewed here aren't intended to be the final word, of course, since each model year brings changes in some standard makes and addition of new designs. However, with minor modifications, it seems likely that many of the models discussed will still be offered by bike builders for a good many years to come. To find exact models currently available, consult the latest catalogs.

The current roster reflects one major trend in recent years: industry emphasis on the dual-purpose bike. The idea is to provide one bike that can be used for two different kinds of riding. Is that good? Cycle builders say it's great. A great many experienced cyclists say it's great for the manufacturers (their sales prove it), but not for the users.

A dual-purpose bike is too much like a ''something for nothing'' concept. You pay for a street bike and supposedly get an off-road one, or vice versa. However, the needs for each category vary so much you don't get the best bike for either use.

Should you completely rule out a dual-purpose bike? That depends. If you're definitely committed to off-road riding primarily, you should buy a bike designed from the start for that. If you plan to use the bike only in town or for transportation, definitely get a full street bike. If you want to do both, the perfect approach is to buy two bikes. Since you probably can't afford that, you might consider a dual-purpose model.

One recent development that helps in that latter case is the increased sophistication of dual-purpose models. Many manufacturers now offer bikes slanted toward one particular use, but with some capability for the other. An example is Kawasaki's tandem of a G-4 "woods" bike and a G-5 "trails" model. If you just glance at these two 100-cc lightweights side-by-side in a showroom, you might think they're twins. But if you review engineering details, you'll find noticeable differences. The G-4 engine housing turns out to be larger, with more fins than the "trails" powerplant, the extra fin area providing better cooling. That's a strong hint that the G-4 is designed more for off-road use than street operation. The added cooling is important if the bike has to slow down when moving over rougher than usual terrain.

You'll also find a variation in gearing. The G-5 trails model has a standard five-speed gearbox while the woods version has a 10-speed system obtained through the use of two reduction gears. When the bike is completely at rest (that is, you don't shift to the reduction gears on the fly), you engage them by moving a lever on the handlebar. When they're moved into place, they lower the gear ratios of the basic-five gear system by 20 percent each. Coupled with modifications of the engine port design to give you extra torque, this is intended to give the extra pulling power needed to make the bike run reasonably well under rugged conditions, such as twisting trails or soggy, muddy going.

There are other variations as well. The G-4 handlebars are narrower than the G-5 to permit maneuvering through narrow openings in tree-lined paths or other tight squeezes. They also tilt back slightly more to make it more comfortable when you operate it from a sitting position. Saddle shape and deflection also are varied from the G-4 to the G-5 as are peg positions for the two applications.

Kawasaki's 100cc G-4 model is an enduro designed more for off-road than street operation.

The tire selection also changes from the G-4 to the G-5. The G-4 uses deep-cleated knobby tires, a pattern selected to provide a firm grip on grass, pine needles, dirt, and the like. Knobby tires are generally poor for streets. They don't hold pavement well (particularly if the ground is wet), wear out rapidly compared to conventional street tires, and give a jarring ride. Conversely, rib-tread or diamond tires designed for pavement have poor holding properties on off-road routes. To get around this, the G-5 has "universal" tires, tires having knob patterns, but with the knobs not as pronounced as on an off-road type and with less space between them to give reasonable (if not the most efficient) holding properties for both off-road areas and on the street.

Most off-road bikes use two-stroke engines for maximum reliability in remote areas. Thus both the G-4 and G-5 incorporate such engines, in this case single-cylinder designs with the rotary disk valve favored by Kawasaki. Both models are rated at 11 HP at 7,500 RPM with a compression ratio of 7:1 and having a bore and stroke, respectively, of 49.8 x 51.8 mm. Top speed for either model is given as 58 MPH, though tests indicate 55 MPH a more normal value. The G-4, with a more rugged frame and a luggage rack, weighs 209 pounds compared to a trimmer 195 pounds for the G-5.

Apart from the question of how perfect either model is for a particular type of riding, an objection must be voiced against the bike designations. Using the words "woods" and "trails" increases consumer confusion at bike-buying time. In the past you knew what was meant by a trails bike or a dirt bike—the terms, which were interchangeable, defined a cycle intended almost exclusively for off-road riding. Now a trails bike, by Kawasaki's or some other manufacturer's definition, may be anything from a full off-road model to a semistreet type. So you have to make sure exactly what type of bike it is you're considering. Make sure the dealer verifies that a particular model is a pure street bike, a pure off-road cycle or something in-between. (Unless you're looking for a racer, which is another matter).

Before examining more lightweights, let's take a brief look at the minibike field. For the most part, you don't have to worry much about pros and cons of dual-purpose in the case of minis. Almost all minibikes are intended for limited riding that doesn't require the performance levels for either extended street or all-out trails riding. However, this may change in future years as designers continue to upgrade the minis. Engineers already have vastly improved the class and recently some street legal designs began to appear.

Many of the early minis looked more like toys than cycles and were treated as such by many dealers and buyers. But in a short while designers worked to make this bike class into true motorcycles just built to smaller scale than other machines. In fact, the newer models have become known as minicycles rather than minibikes.

Young riders developed skills on the new models so rapidly that by the early 1970s the American Motorcycle Association set up a new youth division, now known by the acronym Y-AMA. The Y-AMA now monitors the new sport of minicycle racing for age groups ranging from preteens to early teens. By the mid-1970s, the AMA began issuing a rules book covering more than a dozen minicycle events, including trails, motocross, hillclimb, short track and road racing for 50- and 100-cc classes. Before long, cycle makers were offering racing minicycles as precision-made as the finest standard-size competition bikes—and with prices to match. Some examples of minis built specifically for racing are the Barnt 100MX, Holder Motocross 100 and the Yamaha YZ-80. Prices for these in the mid-1970s ranged from a low of about $454 for the YZ-80 to roughly $1,000 for the Barnt.

The Barnt, designed to take a variety of engines, typically uses a two-stroke, single-cylinder powerplant providing 15 HP at 9,500 RPM. Engine displacement is 98 cc. The dimensions include a wheelbase of 46.5 inches, 16-inch diameter wire wheels, overall length of 69 inches, seat height of 28.5 and handlebar height of 37.5 inches. Dry weight is 180 pounds.

You'll find such unusual features on the Holder Motocross as leading front forks adjustable to five different positions, a special diaphragm carburetor, and a two-stroke Chrysler industrial engine with 100-cc displacement. The bike has a wheelbase of 48 inches, overall length of 67.5 inches, handlebar height of 37.5 inches, seat height of 26 inches and 17 inch-diameter front wheel and 16 inch-rear. Dry weight is 120 pounds.

The Yamaha boasts a 72-cc two-stroke single-cylinder powerplant and five-speed transmission. Wheelbase is 46.8 inches, overall length 68 inches, handlebar height 35.5 inches, seat height 26.5 inches with wheel diameters of 16 inches in front and 14 inches in the rear.

You don't have to be a racing buff to find plenty of minibikes or minicycles to suit your tastes. The brand names in the general mini field include just about all the world's bike builders, including series from Italy's Benelli and Montese; Japan's major companies (Honda, Kawasaki, Suzuki and Yamaha); and others such as Arco, Fox, Holder, Muskin and Rockford. United States entries are from Harley-Davidson and the reborn Indian marque. The Indian minis, introduced by the late, well-known cycle expert Floyd Clymer at the end of the 60s, are credited with being the first of the class to enter the market.

Few of the minis have been street legal. That is, they do not meet the requirements for registration and licensing of bikes for use in normal traffic. Actually, most minis have been designed to avoid registration. One approach has been to use engines with horsepower ratings under the licensing minimum. (Most state licensing laws exempt bikes with less than 5 HP.)

But with rising interest in minis, street legal models have been produced. An example is the Fox Tracker, introduced in 1974. The Tracker's two-stroke single-cylinder engine turns out 5.9 HP at 6,000 RPM. Its dimensions are 48-inch wheelbase, length of 69 inches, seat height 29 inches, handlebar height of 35.5 inches and 16-inch diameter front and rear wheels. Dry weight is 127 pounds. One attraction of this mini is a price from $1 to $200 less than the lowest price standard lightweight.

You can find some mini designs intended for age levels well below the teens. Take the Mini-Mini produced by Indian as an example. Used by the mid-1970s in peewee races in some parts of the United States, this design has a dry weight of only 57 pounds and a wheelbase of just 30.5 inches. Diameter of both solid wheels is eight inches, overall length 44 inches, handlebar height 27 inches and seat height 18 inches. The two-stroke, single-cylinder engine, displacement 47 cc, can provide 1.7 HP at 5,000 RPM.

The 1970s minis with the mini-est prices generally have been those in the Arco or Muskin series. The Arco line begins with the 3004 E-Z Rider and the 3504 models (which look more like scooters than conventional cycles) that listed in the mid-1970s for about $130 and $170, respectively. Aimed for off-road use, both have four-stroke, single-cylinder industrial engines, the 3004 using a 127-cc type turning out 3 HP at 3,600 RPM and the 3504 a 148-cc engine providing 3.5 HP at 3,600 RPM. The 3004 has five-inch solid wheels, 37-inch wheelbase, overall length of 47 inches and seat height of 31 inches. Respective figures for the 3504 are 6, 38, 51 and 24 inches.

The Muskin series features a somewhat more rugged frame than the Arco low-cost designs. The economy version, the Muskin Blazer (about $140 list price in 1974), is powered by a four-stroke, single-cylinder 127-cc engine turning out 3 HP at 3,600 RPM. Wheelbase is 32.5 inches, seat height 21.5 inches, length 45 inches and handlebar height 30.5 inches. Dry weight is 77 pounds and wheel diameter 6 inches.

Yamaha entries in the minicycle field in the mid-1970s included the GT 80 Mini Enduro and the stripped down, higher performance version of that design, the GT MX; the TY 80 trails; and the previously mentioned YZ-80. The GT 80, one of the bellwethers of the growing minicycle field, came out in an improved model in 1974. It uses a 72-cc piston port two-stroke engine, single cylinder with torque induction, that offers improved performance over the previous 60-cc-powered design. The GT 80, whose engine provides a maximum torque of 4 foot-pounds at 6,000 RPM, can achieve a maximum speed of over 47 MPH and has a range close to 100 miles on its 1.3-gallons fuel capacity. The bike weighs 126 pounds, has an overall length of 63.4 inches, seat height of 25.6 inches, wheelbase of 41.1 inches and wheel size of 15 inches front and 14 inches rear. The TY 80 uses an engine basically the same as the GT 80, but modified to produce more torque (4.5 foot-pounds at 5,000 RPM) for off-road needs. Like the others in this line, it has a four-speed transmission. Dimensions include wheelbase of 40.4 inches, overall length of 61.4 inches, seat height of 23.2 inches and handlebar height of 35 inches. Dry weight is 119 pounds.

Suzuki minis in the mid-1970s covered a range from the 49-cc TS-50L to the RV-125L model with 123-cc displacement. The only model not designed primarily for trail use is the TM-75L competition model with a 72-cc single-cylinder two-stroke rotary-valve engine providing 5 HP at 6,000 RPM. The TS-50L, a five-speed transmission design with a two-stroke single cylinder engine, can achieve 4.8 HP at 8,000 RPM. The 125L is one of two in the RV, or Recreational Vehicle minicycle series offering unusually good hill-climbing ability. The other, the 90L, uses an 88-cc two-stroke single-cylinder engine providing 7.8 HP at 6,000 RPM.

The 123-cc RV-125L powerplant turns out 9.8 HP at 6,000 RPM. The 90L has a four-speed transmission and the 125L a five-speed one. Wheelbase and overall length of the 90L are 46.5 and 71.1 inches, respectively, and the 125L, 51.4 and 77.2 inches. The rugged design and precision workmanship is reflected in the $550-$700 price range for these two.

Kawasaki's entries in the minicycle field include the MC-1 enduro off/on road design and the strictly off-road MC-1M. Both are powered by 89-cc, single-cylinder, rotary-disk valve engines providing 6.5 HP at 6,500 RPM. Both have five-speed transmissions with telescopic front-fork suspension and swing-arm rear suspension. Overall width, height, and wheelbase are the same for both: 30.1, 37.2 and 43.3 inches. The MC-1 has an overall length of 68.1 inches and the MC-1M, 65.6 inches. The MC-1M is stripped down to provide a lighter weight of 150 pounds versus 165 for the MC-1. Both models have magneto ignition systems and tank capacities of 1.6 gallons.

The most extensive array of models in the minibike/minicycle class has long been offered by Honda. The grouping ranges from the smallest Honda made, the QA-50K2, to the 89.5-cc CT-90K5. The QA-50K2 is a solid wheel (5-inch diameter) 84-pound minibike with automatic transmission, which is one of the most widely used models in minibike instruction programs. Selling for under $300 (as of 1976), it also is the lowest priced Honda model. Its dimensions include a wheelbase of 34.4 inches, overall length of 47.2 inches, and seat height of 32.9 inches. Also using a 49-cc engine is the Z50AK5, which weighs in at 117 pounds* and offers folding handlebars for ease of storage in trunk or station wagon. This minibike has a three-speed transmission and dimensions of 35.2-inch wheelbase, eight-inch-diameter wheels, 51.2 inch overall length, seat height of 24.8 inches and handlebar height of 33.2 inches.

Ranking among the most popular small cycles, providing compactness and higher performance than the 50-cc models are the CT-70 and XL-70 Hondas. The CT-70 is intended for trail use with fat tires, upswept muffler and spark arrester, while the XL-70 is a dual street/trail design. Both use four-stroke single-cylinder 72-cc engines with the CT-70 incorporating a

*As of 1976, the QA-50 was phased out of production, making the Z50 the smallest Honda in the regular line. We should also note that the "K" designations, which indicated the specific modification of a basic type, were dropped from 1976 on. Instead, year designations (*e.g.*, Z50A-76) for a specific model change were used.

The XL-70 enduro is one of the most popular of the Honda small cycles.

three-speed, automatic-clutch transmission, and the XL-70, a four-speed system. The CT-70 has a wheelbase of 41.3 inches, overall length of 50.6 inches, seat height of 29.1 inches and handlebar height of 39.8 inches. Both wheels are solid types, 10 inches in diameter. The wheelbase of the XL-70 is 43.3 inches, overall length 67.5 inches, seat height 26.5 inches, and handlebar height 37.2 inches. The wire wheels measure 16 inches in diameter in front and 14 inches in back.

The largest minicycle Hondas are the ST-90 and CT-90K5, both of which are classed as standard lightweight bikes rather than minis on some lists. Both have 89-cc, four-stroke, single-cylinder engines, and both are intended for dual street/trail use. Both provide an automatic clutch, but the ST-90 incorporates a three-speed transmission, while the CT-90 goes to four speed. The wheelbase for the ST-90 is 46.1 inches, wheel diameters 14 inches each, seat height 30.3 inches, handlebar height 40.6 inches, and overall length 69.1. Dry weight is 190 pounds. The CT-90 is 73.6 inches long with a wheelbase of 48 inches, seat height of 30.5 inches, handlebar height of 41.3, and dry weight of 198 pounds.

Like the minis, lightweight cycles have come a long way in a short time. Less then ten years after the appearance of the pioneering Honda step-through lightweight, the number of different small cycle models available from manufacturers accounted for more space in a typical buyer's guide than all larger bikes combined. The first Honda lightweight was the forerunner of many models for street transportation that now run the gamut from limited street cycles to powerful high-speed designs. Within a few years after lightweight street bikes found favor with the general public, models engineered for other applications—off-road, racing and enduros—came along. The word *enduro* is the generic term for the dual-purpose street/trail motorcycle.

Though once laughed at by cycle purists, lightweights now are accepted as desirable candidates for all these uses. Because lightweights provide reasonable and even exceptional performance for relatively low cost, knowledgable observers feel they currently meet the requirements of the greatest number of riders. Still, you'll find categories where small cycles just can't provide either the power or the overall strength of the big bikes. Thus, at this writing, there are no lightweight models seriously vying for the touring or sports bike classes. (Sports bikes are also known as day cruisers.)

In the mid-1970s, just about all street models with engine displacements of 125 cc or less were provided by Japanese firms. Designs having sub-100-cc engines include the Kawasaki G-3 90, Suzuki TS-50L Gaucho, and Yamaha RD 60. The Gaucho's 49-cc, two-stroke, rotary-valve, single-cylinder engine provides performance comparable to considerably larger engines of the 1960s. Road tests indicate it can give you up to 70 miles per gallon (MPG) and speeds of 45–50 MPH. Horsepower output is 4.8 at 5,000 RPM. Wheelbase is 46.7 inches, and dry weight 156 pounds. The bike has a five-gear transmission. Yamaha's RD 60 offers a smooth running, two-stroke, single-cylinder engine with 55-cc displacement and compression ratio of 6.9:1 that can provide a top speed of 50 MPH and endurance of 55 MPG. Other features include a five-gear transmission, kick starting in any gear and a flip-open seat with a key-locking latch. Wheelbase is 46.7 inches and dry weight 163 pounds.

Kawasaki's G-3 has an 89-cc displacement, two-stroke, rotary-valve, single-cylinder engine with a compression ratio of 7:1 that provides 10 HP at 7,500 RPM. As the model number indicates, this is a relative of the G-4 and G-5 woods-trails bikes, but it doesn't have the upswept exhaust pipe those require and its gearing is designed for normal street use. The G-3 weighs in at 178 pounds, 20-30 pounds less than its big brothers, which helps it to reach higher speeds (top speed about 62–63 MPH) even though the engine is a little smaller.

Street models in the 125-cc bracket include such designs as Honda's CB-125 Sl and CL-125 Sl and Jawa's CZ 125. The original home of the CZ is Czechoslovakia, and the Jawa bikes from that country have made a proud name for themselves in racing, particularly motocross. In the mid-1970s, Jawa set up its American Jawa affiliate to produce several models, including the 125 street model. The 12-horsepower output at 5,950 RPM of the two-stroke, single-cylinder engine (8.6:1 compression ratio) provides a top speed of about 66 MPH.

Both the Honda 125s are powered by 122-cc, four-stroke, single-cylinder engines with 9.5:1 compression ratios that provide enough punch so the bikes can carry a passenger as well as the driver at reasonable speeds. Both models have foot pegs for two riders. The difference is that the CL-125 Sl has some things in its design giving it some performance for a limited amount of off-road riding. These include a higher placed frame to allow more ground clearance and a transmission

75

arrangement to give some added torque for better hill-climbing. A prospective CL-125 S1 buyer has to decide whether the somewhat better backcountry ability, not really enough for any intensive trails activity, is worth a slightly lower speed capability of 62 MPH vs 66 for the CB-125. This is an example, on a small scale, of some of the tradeoffs you must consider in choosing a mount.

It's worth stressing that while the top speed of typical lightweight bikes might sound ample for all your transportation needs, experts would call all the models discussed above nonexpressway designs. The prime question when you consider a bike for use on superhighways is whether it can keep up with the traffic over long stretches of nonstop roadway.

You'll generally find that the normal cruise speed of a bike is from 10 to 20 percent lower than its maximum speed. A motorcycle with a 12 HP engine and a stated top speed of 62–66 MPH would thus have a cruise speed in the 50–60 MPH range. Even with superhighway speeds lowered to 55 MPH, such a bike speed is marginal at best even if cars stay within posted limits. But realistically, traffic tends to go 5–10 MPH above whatever the law allows and therefore a bike with a cruise speed of 50–60 MPH is underpowered for expressway/freeway operation.

So if you want to do a lot of superhighway riding, you need a bike with enough power to cruise at 65–75 MPH. There may be one or two lightweights that come close and the picture may change tomorrow thanks to new engineering breakthroughs. But for now, bikes providing the needed performance have engines of 175 cc or more turning out from 20–40 HP and are beyond the scope of this book. All the lightweight street bikes discussed above have reasonable performance for other street operations, though.

The majority of lightweight buyers in the mid-1970s, according to industry figures, chose dual-use enduros. We've already expressed our reservations about this type bike. Assuming your decision is to go this route, you'll have to do a lot of head scratching to get the best enduro for your needs. For starters, you first must decide which ratio of street to trail capability you want; values range from 80–20 through 50–50 to 20–80 with percentages in between. This narrows it down to a group of models you can compare on performance and cost bases.

You won't find a lack of candidates. All the familiar Japanese firms have entries as well as such other famous builders as Harley-Davidson,

Indian, Hodaka, Benelli, Sweden's Monark series, Germany's DKW, Bultaco of Spain and the Penton cycles made by Austria's KTM Company.

The 90-cc (and lower) group includes Harley-Davidson's Z-90 and Indian's ME 76–70. The Honda CT-90K5, noted earlier in minicycles, also fits in here. The Z-90 incorporates some of the rugged design the United States firm applies to its better known big bikes. Weighing 184 pounds dry, it has a two-stroke 90-cc, single-cylinder engine that turns out 8 HP and has a 9.2:1 compression ratio. It has a four gear transmission, 46.5-inch wheelbase and top speed of 55 MPH. Indian's ME 76, a United States design built in Taiwan, can hit 55 MPH on the street and has good road-holding properties on dirt. Road tests indicate the 70-cc displacement two-stroke single-cylinder engine (9:1 compression ratio; 8 HP output at 7,500 RPM) can achieve phenomenal fuel economy, providing 90 to 100 MPG. With a 1.6-gallon fuel tank, this means a maximum range of close to 160 miles.

In the 100-cc dual-purpose category are to be found bikes by such firms as Harley-Davidson (SR-100), Hodaka, Honda (XL-100), Kawasaki (G-4 and G-5 described earlier), Penton (Berkshire), Suzuki (TS-100L and TC-100L) and Yamaha (DT-100).

The Harley SR-100 once was called the Baja, a reference to the bike's prize-winning performance in its class in the bone-jarring Baja 1000 desert race in Mexico's Baja California. The 98-cc, two-stroke, single-cylinder engine (50x50 mm bore and stroke with a compression ratio of 9.5:1) turns out enough power for a top speed of 62 MPH. Off-road features include a high-energy absorbing Ceriani front fork, heavy-duty rear shocks, good ground clearance and a five-gear-wide ratio transmission.

Honda's XL-100 is one of the most widely used enduros. As its semiknobby tires, upswept exhaust pipe with spark arrester and five-gear transmission indicate, it is engineered on the 65 percent trail–35 percent street side of things. The 99-cc four-stroke overhead cam, single-cylinder engine, which has a 9.5:1 compression ratio, can turn out an estimated 11.5 HP. Other specs include wheelbase of 50 inches, 19-inch front tire and 17-inch rear, and dry weight of 205 pounds.

The Penton Berkshire is a high-performance cycle usable for normal transportation, but essentially designed for competition as is its close

77

relation, the 100 Berkshire MX (for Motocross) model. The Berkshire offers a 98-cc, two-stroke, single-cylinder engine (48 x 54 mm bore and stroke, 10:1 compression ratio) that can produce a healthy 19 HP at 7,800 RPM. The design, with semiknobby tires, has a wheelbase of 55 inches, dry weight of 208 pounds, speed of 65 MPH and a price befitting its high-quality construction of over $1,000. The MX version has the same power output, but uses a specially modified Sachs DKW type engine with such things as steel rims, magnesium hubs and plastic fenders providing strength with minimum weight.

Suzuki's TS-100L Honcho and TC-100L Blazer are time-tested models, updated to some extent in the mid-1970s, which offer varying degrees of street/trail performance. The Honcho gives you more efficient street-operating capabilities than trail performance, while the Blazer's 2 x 4 transmission effectively provides eight gear speeds to give the low-end range needed for good trail handling. Both models are powered by two-stroke rotary valve single-cylinder engines rated at 18.8 HP at 7,000 RPM (89 cc, 6.5:1) compression ratio). Both use magneto ignition and have upswept exhausts, though the Blazer provides more overall ground clearance. Wheelbase is 49 inches for both models and the Blazer at 205 pounds is three pounds heavier than the Honcho.

The Yamaha DT-100 enduro, which debuted in 1974, borrowed a number of features from the highly successful lightweight Yamaha motocross racer, the MX-100, including a sturdy-frame design and a two-stroke reed-valve induction single-cylinder engine developing an estimated 8.5 HP. The advantage claimed for the reed valve installation is the ability for the bike to reach higher power levels at lower RPM. The DT-100 engine has a displacement of 97 cc, bore and stroke of 52 x 45 mm, compression ratio of 6.8:1 and speed of 58 MPH. It has five gears, weighs 188 pound dry and has a wheelbase of 50.4 inches. The motocross design has a higher compression ratio, 7.8:1, knobby tires (19 inches front and 18 inches rear as on the DT-100) and a weight of 176 pounds.

Moving over to the 125-cc ranks, you'll find almost every major bike manufacturer has a dual-use model in this class, as well as racers that usually are close relatives of the enduro designs. No attempt will be made here to detail the several dozen models in large scale production in the mid-1970s, but a range of designs will be covered to give some feel for the variety and performance capabilities.

Yamaha calls its DT 100B a street legal motorcross machine. The 97cc two-stroke engine can provide a maximum torgue of 7 feet per pound at 7,000 RPM and a maximum speed of over 58 MPH.

Examples of some famous European entrants in this category are Benelli, Bultaco, DKW, Monark and Puch. Benelli's 125 Panther is a direct descendant of its very popular street bike of the early 1970s, the Sprite. It is powered by a 121-cc two-stroke single-cylinder engine (56 x 49 bore and stroke) with a compression ratio of 9.8:1 and a power output of around 10–11 HP. It uses modified knobby tires to give dirt capability (21 inch front and 18 inch back), has five gears, 51-inch wheelbase, dry weight of 210 pounds and speed of 66 MPH. Fuel efficiency is somewhere in the 40–44 MPG range and tank capacity is two gallons.

Bultaco, a famous name in motorcycle racing for many years, presented several improved enduro models in the mid-1970s, the smallest being the Alpina 125, powered by a 124-cc two-stroke, single-cylinder engine with 10:1 compression ratio turning out 11.2 HP at 5,500 RPM. Other details include a magneto ignition system, five-gear transmission, 52.3-inch wheelbase, knobby tires (21 inch front, 18 inch rear), dry weight of 213 pounds and speed of 55 MPH. Bultaco's racing version in this class, the Pursang 125, has a specially designed two-stroke engine with a 14:1 compression ratio that provides 25.4 HP at 10,000 RPM. Other features include a Motoplat electronic ignition system, highly efficient silencer and a dry weight of 192 pounds.

The DKW line in the mid-1970s included four 125-cc models: two dual models also used in competition; and two essentially for racing alone. The two enduros, the 125 Boondocker and 125 Enduro are almost identical, except for the use of leading link forks in the Enduro for improved riding over very rough terrain. Both use a 125-cc two-stroke single-cylinder German-made engine with a 12:1 compression ratio providing 24 HP at 7,000 RPM and a top speed of 65 MPH. Both have six gears and weigh roughly 218 pounds. Both use Motoplat electronic ignition as do the other 125s in the line, the 125 Hornet (a strong competitor in desert racing) and the 125 Motocross. The main difference between the Motocross and Hornet is the use of leading link forks.

The candidate of Sweden's Monark cycle firm in the mid-1970s for 125-cc honors is the 125 Six-Day Replica. The name indicates the design is a duplicate of a gold medal winning bike ridden by Swedish experts in the 1973 ISDT. The cycle uses a 123-cc two-stroke single-cylinder engine, with a 13:1 compression ratio, providing 24 HP at 8,500 RPM. It has Motoplat electronic ignition, six gears, 52-inch wheelbase, weighs

202 pounds and can reach a speed of 72. It is one of the few lightweights that you might consider for freeway operation. The Monark family includes two 123-cc motocross racers, the 125 MX with a two-stroke, single-cylinder engine (12:1 compression ratio) turning out 21 HP at 8,500 RPM and the 125 MX GS with a 15:1 compression ratio providing 25 HP at 9,200 RPM.

Winning friends in the 1970s was the Puch 125 Enduro, a product of the Austrian Puch company, which started building motorcycles in 1899. (Puch also produces a 125 Motocross bike, essentially the same as the Enduro except for some detailed modifications). The 124-cc two-stroke single-cylinder engine has a 13.8:1 compression ratio, Bosch electronic ignition and can provide 23 HP at 8,500. Wheelbase is 54 inches, dry weight 209 pounds and speed about 65 MPH.

Turning to some of the Japanese 125-cc entries, Kawasaki offers the KS 125 street/trail model and KX 125 Motocross. The engines for both are almost identical, but the racer has special long-travel shocks and the angle the front fork makes with the horizontal (called the rake angle) is steeper, measuring about 31 degrees against about 26 for the enduro.

The Motocross naturally emphasizes lighter weight, coming in at 195 pounds dry against 214 pounds for the KS 125. The engine in both cases is a two-stroke single-cylinder rotary-valve type with a compression ratio of 8:1. The KS 125 has magneto ignition, while the KX 125 uses Capacitor Discharge Ignition (CDI). Both have six speed transmission. The KX 125 specs include wheelbase of 52 inches, overall length of 79.5 inches and overall height of 44.1, telescopic front fork suspension and swing arm rear fork suspension, fuel tank capacity 1.7 gallons. The KS details include wheelbase of 53 inches, overall length of 82 inches, overall height of 42.9 inches with a two-gallon fuel tank.

Honda's series includes the XL-125 and MT-125 enduros and CR-125M motocross/off road bike. The MT-125 is one of the rare Hondas to use a two-stroke engine instead of a four. The model has a compression ratio of 7:1, 56 x 50 mm bore and stroke, and a five-gear transmission. It uses semiknobby tires, 21 inch front and 18 inch rear, weighs 207 pounds dry, has a 54-inch wheelbase and a top speed of about 60 MPH. The XL-125 is powered by a 122-cc four-stroke overhead-cam single-cylinder engine (56 x 49.5 mm bore and stroke) 9.3:1 compression ratio, which can take the bike to speeds of 60 MPH. Weight is 214 pounds dry. The bike has a five-gear transmission and wheelbase of 52 inches. The CR-125M is stripped down to 179 pounds for racing, has a high strength, lightweight chrome-moly alloy steel frame and CDI.

Suzuki's 125s include the TS-125L Duster, the TC-125SL Prospector and the highly regarded TM-125L motocross model, the Challenger. More than any other model, the Duster provides adjustments that theoretically let you get ready for almost any kind of terrain. These features include front forks you can adjust to three positions and shock absorbers with five alternative loadings. The 123-cc two-stroke single-cylinder engine (56 x 50 mm bore and stroke, 6.7:1 compression ratio) generates 12.7 HP at 7,000 RPM. Weight is 198 pounds, wheelbase 51.6 inches and speed 65 MPH.

The Prospector, as the name implies, is slanted more for trail riding than street use. It has a 2 x 4 transmission, giving eight speeds. The engine is essentially the same as for the Duster. Dimensions are about the same, but the Prospector weighs about 10 pounds more.

The Challenger provides a robust 17.5 HP at 10,000 RPM from its two-stroke single-cylinder 123-cc engine. It uses Capacitor Discharge Ignition and has a ratio of 7.5:1. The engines can develop a torque of 9.68 foot-pounds at 8,000 RPM. Wheelbase is 52.6 inches and weight 189 pounds.

Yamaha's 125s comprise the all-purpose DT 125 and the motocross models MX 125 and YZ 125. The DT 125 features a battery and coil ignition system for quick starting and a good power margin for both street and trail use. The engine for all three models is a two-stroke single-cylinder reed-valve type, but compression ratio is 7.1:1 for the Enduro and 8:1 for the racers. Both racers make wide use of aluminum and plastic parts to minimize weight. Thus the YZ 125 weighs in at 176 pounds against 233 pounds for the DT 125.

Last but not least in this brief roundup is the Hodaka family ranging from the 98-cc Dirt Squirt to the 125 Wombat and Combat Wombat. The Combat Wombat is the racing version of the 125 Wombat, considered one of the most reliable and durable lightweights on the market. The 125 Wombat, well designed for trail use with ground clearance of 11 inches and modified knobbies, has an unusually large fuel tank holding 2.7 gallons. Its 123-cc two-stroke single-cylinder engine can provide an estimated level of over 12 HP at 7,500 RPM. It has five gears, 53-inch

Widely used in motocross racing, the Suzuki TM-125 Challenger offers a power level of 17.5 horsepower at 10,000 RPM.

wheelbase, 208 pounds dry weight and speed of 65 MPH. The Combat Wombat weighs roughly 16 pounds less than the 125 Wombat and has a compression ratio of 8:1 compared to 7.2:1 for the other design. It attains max horsepower at 8,400 RPM.

All in all, as a prospective buyer you don't have to look far to find all the small cycle capabilities your heart desires. It might help to have a pocket computer handy to figure out which combination of properties matches your dream spectrum. And once you've made your choice and are happily piling up the mileage, the only important thing remaining is to be able to keep your pride and joy running smoothly.

5

KEEPING IT RUNNING

Having a motorcycle is one thing, keeping it running another. The great majority of bikes on the market today are engineered to provide you with a long period of trouble-free riding. For the most part, they are designed to take a considerable amount of load and vibration beyond normal wear-and-tear from road or trail with minimum effect on the major systems.

However, this doesn't mean you should go out of your way to exceed normal operating standards. The answer to gaining long, reliable service from even the most ruggedly built bike is for you to apply tender loving care.

Besides avoiding doing things beyond a bike's capability, you should have some idea of what to look for to keep it in good condition. You should, in effect, practice "preventive" maintenance. This means constant examination of as many major systems as possible to detect potential problems before they grow to the point that major breakdowns occur. It also means being familiar with the owner's manual and following instructions about the timing of particular maintenance steps.

Equally important is your piling up enough hours running your cycle so you'll sense immediately if the bike isn't operating as it should. Before reaching that point, though, you can get a head start in several ways. Learning maintenance basics in a good bike-instruction course is one of these. Another is studying literature on trouble-shooting, and a third is

What you do off a bike can determine how well you do on it. Preventative maintenance and a knowledge of trouble-shooting can go far towards assuring you long, problem-free riding.

discussing preventive maintenance considerations with experienced bike mechanics.

If you intend to do some extensive off-road riding, besides practicing good preventive maintenance, it's essential that you be able to perform a number of major repairs on your own. Where a bike is to be operated only in urban areas or not too far from civilization, the situation is different. The more tell-tale signs of trouble the urban cyclist knows the better and, if you can also make indicated adjustments to cure such problems, that is a plus. But it isn't absolutely necessary; in fact, unless you really have mastered specific mechanical techniques, in many cases it's wiser and, in the long run, cheaper to take the bike to a skilled mechanic for repairs.

Some newcomers to cycling get the feeling that the motorcycle is a simple machine because of its compactness and the feeling of individuality it provides. However, in many ways it is more complex than an automobile. To get the desired performance in a small package, bike engineers have had to balance a lot of intricate factors and it can be harder to work on something condensed into smaller space than one as spread out as an automobile.

A good example is the tire system. Tire repairs on the average adult-size bike are far from easy. It takes a lot of dexterity to get a wide diameter, narrow tube back into the tire and the tire onto the rim without accidentally puncturing the tire. Even highly experienced bike shop mechanics may ruin a job and have to do it over, which is why the cost of fixing a tire at a shop is so high.

In fact, while you can learn tire repair on many bikes with concentration and practice, there are some bikes where the disassembly of the wheel from other bike components makes it essentialy impossible for a nonexpert to do it. A good many minibikes, though, have very simple "fat" tire installations that lend themselves to reasonable repair methods. Minibike tire repair procedures, described later in the chapter, involve patching techniques you can apply to any tire system.

From the standpoint of preventive maintenance, you obviously should examine the tires for uneven wear. If you see this, you know the suspension system needs adjusting to correct conditions that could lead to poor cornering, tire blowouts, or other undesirable consequences. Naturally you also want to keep on the lookout for badly worn treads, indicating you need to get new tires. With a new bike, though, you

Good, sharply defined tire treads like this one are devoutly to be wished. If you see uneven wear spots, beware! It probably means the suspension system needs adjustment.

shouldn't have to worry about this (with proper care) until the tires have 15–20,000 miles on them.

If your bike has wire wheels, you should examine the wires and spokes to make sure they are all in place and properly lined up. With a little practice you can conduct a rapid test to make sure the wheel is running true. You can do this by rotating the wheel with the bike supported on the kick stand. Hold the tip of a screwdriver a short distance from the side of the rim. If the installation is correct, this distance should appear to stay exactly the same as the wheel revolves.

There are several easy tests you can perform to make sure the steering head bearing is in good shape. One way is to push the front forks up and down and also turn the wheel from side to side. If the assembly moves easily with no resistance, that indicates that the fork bushings are worn or there is excessive play in the bearing assembly. Carefully tightening up the adjusting nut above the bearing can help cut down the excess play.

A number of things can be checked out with simple instruments, which you can buy for relatively little money if the bike isn't equipped with them. For bikes with a separate oil system, an oil pressure gauge can be helpful. Many of the new models come with an oil-pressure indicator light on the instrument panel that lights up when oil pressure drops below the safe level. The problem is that this only happens after the pressure drops off. From a preventive maintenance standpoint, you will want to detect the problem before you end up stranded on the side of the road. The answer is to use any of several oil-pressure gauges that can let you determine the moment pressure level begins to fall. Some oil temperature gauges also can be used to keep tabs on engine temperature. On dry sump engines, many designs have the gauge built directly into an oil cap and dipstick assembly for the most effective measurement of temperature.

The instrument most helpful in determining the health of the electrical system is the ammeter. You can buy a reasonably good one inexpensively. Again, it gives you forewarning of possible problems whereas a simple indicator light goes on only when the system has stopped working.

When the engine is running, a look at the ammeter will tell you if the bike is generating less or more power than it needs for good operation. If the ammeter needle moves on the positive side, it indicates that the generator is charging and on the negative side that it isn't. If the system isn't charging, it might point to difficulties with the generator, rectifier or, for bikes that have it, the voltage regulator.

You can check other parts of the electrical system just by seeing if they work. This includes turning on the lights, trying the brake-light switch, blowing the horn, seeing if turn signals flash and so on. In addition, you should regularly study all the electrical wires to make sure there are no loose or frayed wires.

Most experts also suggest adding a fuel gauge if the bike doesn't have one. If a bike has a speedometer with an odometer (mileage gauge), the odometer can be used to keep rough track of mileage so you'll know when to fill up the gas tank. However, it's easy to lose count causing you to run out of gas a long way—or an inconvenient one—from a gas station. (There's also the danger that the shock and vibration of riding can degrade the speedometer system, which, in turn, affects the odometer on that instrument.)

One approach is to buy a small, resettable odometer that you set back to zero whenever the tank is filled. Of course, you have to know what kind of mileage your bike is providing to monitor the odometer properly. Since the typical tank only holds a gallon or two, it's important for you to have a pretty precise knowledge of your bike's mileage performance.

Of course, you'll want to monitor the engine closely, which can be a costly item if repairs are needed. Most of today's fresh-from-the-factory powerplants are marvels of rugged operating machinery. But things can go wrong, particularly after you've run the bike a while, and it's a good idea to do some checks from time to time. While you may not have the ability to disassemble an engine completely, there are a number of simple steps you can perform.

One place to start is the ignition points. The owner's manual should show how to remove the cover to get a look at them. The points should have a nice even, unpitted surface with an unbroken metal layer showing. (The metal face is tungsten.) If there are indentations, grooves or other obvious imperfections on the points, it indicates either excessive wear or possibly arcing due to deficiencies in the condenser or coil installation. Whatever the reason, this calls for a trip to the repair shop.

The next step is to pull the spark plug(s) and give them a once-over. You usually can accomplish this easily just by detaching the high-tension cord cap and removing the plug with a spark plug wrench. (The manufacturer generally supplies this in the regular tool kit, although most such kits are inadequate for all requirements and some additions will be suggested later.) The tip of the plug should be inspected for deposits or fouling and the point cleaned, preferably with a spark plug cleaner. If you do not have a cleaner, an alternate way is to use a stiff wire, such as a pin, to remove deposits, then wash the part in solvent and dry with a rag.

Examination of the plug when it's first taken out can provide good insight into the engine's condition. The proper color of the electrodes is a gray or light brown. Should the plugs be black, it indicates problems of combustion. For an engine where oil isn't mixed with gasoline, it might mean the oil rings aren't sealing properly and lubricating oil is getting past them into the cylinder. Or it might point to the need for adjustment to reduce an overly rich fuel-air mixture. On the other hand, the points might be white and eroded in places. This is caused by a very hot combustion chamber temperature that generally results from a lean (too little fuel compared to air volume) mixture. The last situation, allowed to continue over a long time, can cause major damage to valve assemblies. Of course if the plug is chipped or broken you should replace it.

Another inexpensive instrument you can use for preventive maintenance is the compression gauge. The gauge is inserted in the spark plug hole after you remove the plug. Generally, when you perform this test, you need assistance from another person who holds the bike and depresses the kick starter until the cylinder being tested is on the compression stroke. For most bikes, a gauge reading of 150 pounds or more is a healthy one. If you find a reading of 100 pounds or less, it might point to valve or ring problems.

If the problem in engine performance is in the fuel-air ratio, you can take care of this by adjusting the carburetor. But you should first run some other tests to see if the problem lies elsewhere. For instance, Honda Company warns, "Malfunction of the engine at high speed can be caused by a defective ignition or valve system. Therefore, determine the cause of the trouble before attempting to correct the condition by carburetor adjustment."

Assuming tests indicate you do have carburetor ills, here's the Honda routine for the Model CB-125. "Carburetor adjustment should only be made when the engine is at operating temperature. First set the idle speed to 1,200 RPM with the throttle stop screw. Turning the screw clockwise will increase engine speed. Manipulate the air screw to obtain the maximum and stable engine speed. The standard air screw setting is from

1-¾ to 1½ turns open from full-closed position. Readjust the throttle stop screw if it is necessary to reset the idle speed.''

The transmission system usually has to be taken to the overhaul shop if problems arise, because the gearbox is sealed. But you can and should keep watch on parts that can be seen such as the drive shaft assembly. (Obviously you couldn't do this if your bike used a direct drive shaft). The chain should look tight but have a little play in it. The lower section should not seem to droop down. The chain should have a slightly moist look from the lubricant. To determine if the chain is correctly adjusted, you should rest the cycle on its main stand and move the chain up and down at the midpoint between the sprockets. Total movement should be no more than about 0.4 to 0.8 inches. If the slack is more than this, adjust the chain following the instructions in your owner's manual.

Keeping the chain well lubricated and clean is also important to long transmission life. Bike makers strongly recommend that you use commercially prepared chain lubricants rather than ordinary motor oil or other substances. Each chain joint should be saturated so the lubricant penetrates the space between adjacent surfaces of link plates and rollers. Excess oil should be carefully wiped off. When the chain becomes very dirty, you should remove it by detaching the master link, then clean it in solvent and dry. Before you put it back in place, inspect it for any wear or damage. This is also a good time for you to examine the sprocket teeth to make sure they are not badly worn or "hooked." If the sprocket is in poor condition, you should replace it.

Making sure the brakes are in good operating condition naturally is also vital. Bike manufacturers stress that brakes should be checked and adjusted on a regular basis even if you don't notice any problems during normal riding. (Of course, it is important to note any sudden changes in braking performance, which then calls for immediate analysis and remedy.) Taking 2 to 4 hours as a normal "riding day," after an initial check when the first 30 riding days or so are past, it's suggested you examine your brakes at 60 riding day intervals thereafter.

Manual adjustment is needed on shoe-type expansion brakes. Hydraulic disk brakes, used primarily on large bikes at this writing, have provision for self-adjustment through taking additional fluid into the system from the fluid reservoir as the friction pads wear. If you have that type system, you must make sure the brake fluid level in the reservoir is maintained at the proper point and that you examine the disk pads to ensure they haven't worn down too much.

For shoe-type brakes, you have to adjust brake operation to compensate for friction surface wear. The procedure Honda suggests for checking the front brake on the CB125 begins with placing a support block under the engine to raise the front wheel off the ground. You can then spin the wheel by hand and use a ruler to measure the amount the front brake lever must be moved before the brake starts to take hold. The lever free play for this system at the end of the lever should be between 0.8 and 1.2 inches. If too much or too little play is noted, you can accomplish the brake adjustment in two ways. For a small adjustment, a front brake cable adjuster is provided. For greater changes you can turn the front brake adjusting nut on the front brake panel counterclockwise to increase brake lever play or clockwise to decrease it.

The process for checking the rear wheel brake is similar, except that here pedal-free travel is monitored. On the CB125, normal free play, measured at the pedal tip, is on the order of one inch. A rear brake adjusting nut is provided on the rear brake plate to take care of this.

The only 100 percent sure way to check shoe-type brakes is to remove the wheel and look at the linings. This is relatively easy to do on some bikes and involved on others. Unless you've been well schooled in doing this, it may be wiser for you to turn the task over to a mechanic. However, if you have a new bike, you rarely have to worry until considerable time has elapsed. After a bike has piled up 15,000 miles or more on the odometer (assuming the odometer is working properly), it may be worth having the brake lining examined.

The various hand levers sometimes are bent out of shape and if you try to twist them back to the right contour you have to be careful the metal doesn't snap. A broken lever can make it difficult to operate the bike and also can cut your hands. If the amount broken off is small, you can just file the end smooth. Another approach recommended by Honda is to use a bicycle hand brake vinyl lever cover. Before you put it on, you should cover the broken lever with contact cement or weatherstrip adhesive. Slip the cover on while the cement is still sticky.

Whether or not a bike has an automatic transmission, adjustment of the clutch may sometimes be called for. One indication of an improperly positioned clutch is that the bike tends to creep forward when the gear is in neutral. Conversely, if the clutch doesn't fully engage, the bike won't accelerate properly in gear. For most minibikes and lightweight cycles, clutch adjustment can be done simply by turning one or two lock nuts.

A bike with an automatic centrifugal clutch only requires an adjustment in the clutch assembly. For a manual design, you need also to examine the hand lever. In all cases, adjustment is done with the engine turned off. For such automatic centrifugal clutch models as Honda's QA50, Z50A and CT-70, the adjuster lock nut is exposed on one side of the clutch housing.

For these models you first loosen the nut by turning it clockwise with the correct size wrench. Your next turn the adjuster screw counterclockwise about one turn until you feel resistance, after which you slowly back off the screw clockwise about one-eight to one-quarter turn. While holding the screw in position with a screwdriver, you then turn the nut clockwise until it is firmly in place. The engine is then started to make sure it is running smoothly in neutral and idles correctly when the transmission is shifted into first gear.

Some other adjustments that you can do on your own include adjusting valves and ignition timing. In most cases recommended times for this are after the first 200 miles on a new bike and at intervals of 3,000 miles thereafter. (Keeping track of these and other maintenance milestones is important. You would be wise to keep careful records of the dates and mileage for adjustments and service work.) Most tool kits for specific models come with screwdrivers, wrenches and thickness gauges needed for both these tasks.

Taking the Honda CT-70 as an example, the valve adjust operation begins with removal of valve cover plugs and the flywheel cover. Remember that no work on the valves should start until the engine is cold. A minimum of four hours is required after the last operation of the motorcycle. The flywheel is then turned until the ''T'' mark on the wheel lines up with the crankcase index mark. Before proceeding, you have to make sure the piston is at the top of the compression stroke and both valves closed using the method indicated in the maintenance manual (or from instructions gained from dealer mechanics). If the stroke is not correct, the flywheel is turned counter-clockwise one full turn until the two marks line up again.

You then use the thickness gauge to check the clearance between the valve stem and the rocker arm. For all the Honda minis, the space should be 0.002 inches. If the 0.002 leaf on the gauge won't go in, the space is too small; if it goes in too easily, the adjustment is too loose. For proper clearance, says Honda, the leaf should enter with a slight feeling of resistance. If adjustment is needed, the adjuster lock nut is loosened and the adjuster screw turned clockwise or counter-clockwise to remedy the situation. After the proper clearance is obtained, the cover sections are put back firmly in place.

On Honda minibikes, removing the flywheel cover also permits access to the ignition points. The flywheel is rotated until the gap between contact points is greatest and the thickness gauge used to monitor the spacing. If the gap is greater or smaller than 0.012 to 0.016 inch, it should be adjusted as noted in maintenance instructions. However, if your examination of the contact points discloses the gap to be very small or the points pitted or burned off, those parts need to be replaced. You can master this with practice. Until you have the chance to do it a few times under the supervision of a good home mechanic, it's probably better to let the repair shop pull the flywheel.

Timing on the Honda minis is set by rotating the flywheel counter-clockwise until the "F" mark is lined up with a notch on the side of the crankcase. When the marks are aligned, the contact points should be just starting to separate. If this isn't so, loosen the locking screw and insert the point of a screwdriver into the adjusting notch and apply pressure to realign the point positions.

On Honda's regular lightweights, such as the CB125, adjustment is made by loosening two contact breaker plate locking screws and moving the breaker base plate. Moving the plate clockwise will advance the timing, and vice versa. This is done after the breaker point gap has been adjusted. The screws are then retightened. The most precise timing, Honda notes in its CB125 manual, is gained by using a stroboscopic timing light with the engine idling at 1,200 RPM. After adjustments are completed, the covers are refastened.

As we said earlier, except on minis you shouldn't take tire repair lightly; generally it's better left to the bike shop. The instructions for fixing a mini's tire, though, normally apply to any tire repair. Suggested equipment for this includes the proper open end and socket wrenches for removing the wheel and disassembling it, diagonal cutters, scissors, white chalk, a tube patch kit, and a valve core wrench.

After you take the wheel off the bike, the first step is to remove the valve core to deflate the tire, placing a chalk mark on the tire sidewall at the valve stem position. On most minis that use split flange disk wheels, you then take off the bolts holding the flanges on either side of the rim and remove the flanges. The tire bead may be stuck to the rim, in which case you can loosen it by placing the tire on the ground and pressing the heels of your shoes successively around the rim perimeter until the bead comes free. If you're doing the repair at home, you might use a bench vise instead to apply pressure to the tire.

You can then take the tube out of the tire, insert the valve core and inflate the tube. One way to check for air leaks is to run your hand around the tube diameter. Or you might rotate the tube in a pan of water until rising bubbles disclose a leak. (If no leaks can be found in the tube proper, the leak probably is in the valve stem. If so, use a new stem.)

When you find a leak, use the chalk to mark an area larger than should be needed for a patch. Use the kit grater to roughen the surface around the leak, then spread a drop of cement on this section and allow it to dry. Next select a patch, the right size if possible; otherwise you can use the scissors to shape a section of material. Remove the adhesive backing from the patch and press the patch down on the cemented area as symmetrically as possible. After deflating the tube, roll the patch smooth using the kit as a roller. Then reinsert the valve and inflate the tube until it's firm.

Using the chalk mark on the tire sidewall as a guide, you align the tube with the tire and put chalk marks on the tire tread matching the patch area. You should then inspect the tire to find the possible cause of the leak. Nails, metal fragments, and the like, have to be removed, using the diagonal cutters as an aid. If the problem seems to be a rough edge on the inside of the tire, it must be smoothed down. The grater can be used for this. Finally, deflate the tube again, replace it in the tire and reassemble the wheel with the valve stem in place for reinflating.

As with an automobile, the battery should be regularly examined to make sure the proper electrolyte level is maintained. The level generally is marked on the side of the battery, so you can check it visually after removing the side cover of the battery compartment. If the level is too low, remove the proper cell caps and use a small syringe or plastic funnel to add distilled water. From time to time, you should check the specific gravity of the battery electrolyte with a gauge to determine battery condition. For most bike systems, if the reading is below 1.2, the battery either needs recharging or may have to be replaced if it won't hold a charge.

It's obviously important that you have a good selection of tools if you're going to keep your bike running well or for troubleshooting in case of emergency. Since standardization among all bikes produced by the industry is almost unheard of (sometimes wide variations in bolt sizes, screw types, and so on, exist between model series made by the same company), a tool kit suited to all bikes is almost impossible to find. Each model comes with a kit containing tools matched to its specific components, but usually there are wide gaps in the equipment needed to meet major maintenance requirements. Your best approach is to use the original kit as a starting point, then add some important supplementary tools. If you can't figure out what you need from personal experience, you might discuss the matter with friends experienced in bike maintenance.

A typical manufacturer's model kit includes several open-end wrenches, a box wrench or two, various regular and Phillips (cross head) screwdrivers and a spark plug wrench. Good additions for field use include a 6- to 8-inch vise-grip wrench and long-nose pliers with a wire-cutter provision. For the home workshop, tools of interest include crescent wrenches, various sockets for hex-head nuts and bolts, a socket adapter and socket extension; a ratchet handle to permit faster action of sockets; such other handles as the tee handle and flex handle.

You'll also find it handy to have an impact driver for loosening nuts, bolts and screws located in places too tight for conventional tools. Other items worth having include a pair of diagonal cutters and a point file for cleaning spark plug and breaker points. Thickness and spark plug gauges mentioned earlier also should be on hand for ignition system adjustment. Other workshop tools for bike repairs include a light hammer, rubber mallet, flywheel puller and a tire pump.

Besides tools, you must consider such additional necessities as spare parts and other emergency gear if your plans call for a lot of backcountry riding.

6
GOOD RIDING SENSE

Evil Knievel received a rousing ovation from a large group of fans at the Canadian National Exposition near Toronto, Canada, who came to watch his motorcycle show the week before he was scheduled to make his now legendary attempt to ride his "sky cycle" across Idaho's Snake River Canyon.

Before demonstrating some of his daredevil stunts and the riding skills of his two sons, then aged eleven and thirteen, he took a moment to step to the microphone and address the crowd. He wanted everyone to know that while he took some daring chances in his act, when he wasn't "on the job" he believed in obeying the rules of safety for two-wheelers.

"You (cyclists) that are in the stands, remember this. Never ride a motorcycle without a helmet and never do stunts with your bike unless you have professional instruction. Never take any chances!"

Knievel's advice is echoed by almost every top-rank cycle expert from other stunt riders to experienced competition motorcyclists. For 99 percent of all motorcycle use, these riders stay within legal guidelines. They know only too well that abusing the machine or flouting regulations on street or trail riding is a surer way of courting death or serious injury than taking part in the seemingly more dangerous moments of racing or stunt riding. Following the expert's cycling rules, as Knievel puts it, is just "good riding sense."

Few true cycle fans have many good words for unthinking cyclists who disturb neighborhoods with "buzzing" tactics or with ultraloud-sounding bikes. Nor do they support riders who think it's all right to disobey ecological guidelines recommended by the Motorcycle Industry Council or the American Motorcycle Association. Experienced cyclists generally understand that unnecessarily ripping up sensitive countryside can ruin once beautiful regions for generations to come.

Apart from the question of whether it's fair to abuse the rights of others who have done a thoughtless rider no harm, overstepping bounds in public can lead to painful consequences, including spending time in court or paying heavy fines. The latter situation is becoming increasingly possible for offenders as advanced technology provides police with better ways of dealing with unruly cyclists.

An example is the widespread introduction of helicopters into police and sheriff's departments. Captain Terry Jagerson, head of the aviation department of the San Bernardino, California, sheriff's office, notes that a large percentage of complaints from average citizens is about infractions by motorcyclists:

> A few individuals have taken out their hangups on society this way, feeling there was almost no way for them to be caught. It's true that police patrol cars find it almost impossible to catch a motorcycle lawbreaker. But with a high speed helicopter it's a different story. For instance, we had problems with a group of cyclists who annoyed many neighborhoods and thumbed their nose at ground police. The patrol cars called our group in, we tracked the pack down from the air quickly and radioed ahead to ground cars to set up a block. We hovered over the cyclists and used our loudspeakers to tell them to slow down and stop where we wanted them to. They lined up and each got a citation one after the other.

However, there's no doubt that the overwhelming majority of riders have no interest in such activities. But far too many ignore some of the rules of sensible riding which have evolved for the protection—and better enjoyment of cycling—of the rider himself. The word for good riding and uninterrupted savoring of the true pleasures of cycling is "defense": knowing the right ways of riding and riding defensively, always alert for the unexpected from any quarter.

When traveling in traffic even experienced riders sometimes forget

Professional motorcycle racers like Yvon DuHamel know the value of wearing a helmet as does daredevil Evel Knievel. Their advice to all small cycle riders is ''Never ride a motorcycle without a helmet.''

Jim Weinert, shown here racing for Team Kawasaki, would never think of riding his machine without protective equipment—an example all young cyclists should follow.

how small a rider and motorcycle are compared to a car or truck. The less the overall height of the bike, the more difficult it becomes for an automobile driver to see it in traffic.

Thus if you try to take a mini that's basically intended for backyard or trail use onto a main thoroughfare, you're really tempting fate. Even a bike that's reasonably sized for use in traffic may not be a good bet if it doesn't have equipment vital for such operation, including powerful, well-placed lights, turn signals, reflectors, and the right kind of tires. Of course, a bike that isn't fitted out in accordance with state safety laws isn't legal for use in traffic and forgetting this may bring you a costly ticket.

Assuming your bike is not too small for traffic and is street legal, you still have to take precautions. One of the most important is to be well versed in riding basics before attempting to go into traffic. As Yamaha instructors stress in the company's Learn to Ride Safely program, the bike owner should remember that "to be a safe and skillful rider takes practice. Before you do ride in traffic, the operations of your motorcycle should become automatic to you. Don't attempt to ride in the street until you are totally familiar with the required riding skills. Practice in an empty parking lot until you're totally sure of yourself and your machine."

Like learning to swim, you should gain experience in traffic by first "getting your feet wet," then venturing a little further as time goes by. That is, it's a good idea to start on local streets where traffic is light, then gradually extend your trips to more and more highly traveled roadways. And you should stay away from freeways and expressways unless you know your bike has the performance needed to keep up with the fast-moving traffic.

It's also to your advantage to use everything possible to bring your presence to the attention of cars and trucks. One way you can do this is to wear brightly colored clothing that will stand out no matter what the time of day; the time-honored black motorcycle jacket obviously doesn't meet this criterion.

Cycle experts also urge strongly that you keep your bike's headlights on whenever you're on the road, day and night. A legal street bike also should have a powerful horn. Don't be afraid to use it whenever another vehicle is getting too close or performing a maneuver that indicates the driver might not see you.

A mini-enduro like this one is fun to ride, but it's not designed for expressway use.

We've stressed it before, but can never stress too much that your clothing should not only be noticeable, it should be the best possible for maximum protection. It should be comfortable, and also cover all parts of your body from toes to head to prevent injury in case of a fall and to protect you against bad weather or flying objects. If you wear boots, they should be made of durable leather and have tops that extend above your ankles. If you use shoes instead, they should be high top and have heavy soles.

And most important of all, as Evel Knievel stresses, you need the right kind of head protection. You should get a helmet that fits comfortably and meets American National Standard Z-90.1. There are some who'll tell you it's a waste of time and comfort using a helmet. But a 1974 study by the National Highway Traffic Administration indicates otherwise. The information it collected, says NHTA, shows that cyclists "who do not wear safety helmets are nearly three times as likely to suffer serious or fatal injuries in a crash as are those who wear the protective headgear." Comparisons of motorcycle accidents in Michigan, where the law requires wearing a helmet, with Illinois, which doesn't, showed fatal or serious head injuries are lower in Michigan by 62 percent.

But the best reason for you to wear a helmet is your own self-interest. The rewards of cycling come from riding, not being trussed up in bandages in some hospital room.

In choosing a helmet, quality, condition and design of the helmet is important. From its studies, NHTA suggests you should get one that fits correctly and that is held in place with the right kind of strap. The things that appear to cause most cycling head injuries, says NHTA, are: a failure of the strap system under impact, a strap that was fastened too loosely, or the rider's forgetting to fasten the strap.

Let's assume your clothing is the right type, you have on a strong helmet with good goggles and you're on your way down the highway. Now you should concentrate on riding defensively. A first principle in this is to keep on the left-hand side of your highway lane. This won't make you particularly popular with many motorists. Some drivers, indeed, angrily may try to signal you to move to the right to make passing easier for them. But you have to remember that legally, you have the right to the full lane just as any motorist has and you also have the right to health and happiness, which might be jeopardized if you heed the "move over"

109

urging of a four-wheeler. In all fairness, the motorist doesn't realize how important it usually is for you to be "left-oriented." But in the middle of traffic, there's no way for you to educate the other party.

To begin with, keeping in the left-tire track of the car ahead automatically keeps you out of the center of the lane. That part of the lane is the most treacherous for a motorcycle because it's where any oil or fluid leaking from a car will be deposited. Such a pattern of oil and grease won't bother another automobile, but it could cause your motorcycle to slip and swerve.

A second point: assuming the driver in the car ahead has the proper rearview mirrors and uses them, you'll help ensure that he sees you by riding in the left part of the lane. However, you never can assume that driver will use his mirrors, so riding too close is at least as poor an idea for you as for an automobilist.

Actually, tailgating is far more dangerous for the cyclist. You don't have one to three tons of metal around you to absorb impact force if the car up front stops short. So defensive riding calls for staying far enough behind to allow stopping room if something goes wrong. Yamaha experts suggest that in swiftly moving traffic you should leave two to three motorcycle lengths distance for each 10 MPH of speed. On freeways, a little extra is desirable.

You also want to ride to the left for another reason: the traffic in back of you. When you're on the left, it forces vehicles to go around you to pass. If the driver behind you starts honking and you move to the right to make passing easier for him, the car might crowd you even farther to the right. If an obstacle suddenly loomed up, such as someone in a parked car opening a door, you then would have no room to maneuver. It would mean you'd either have to ram into the obstacle or swerve to the left into the side of the fast moving passing car. Options like this help show why left is right.

The left-hand position also makes sense if you consider the possible action of a vehicle in back of the one right behind you. If your bike is to the right on a multilane highway, the second driver may not realize you're there until he tries to pull back into the lane after passing the car in back of you. Once again, the possible result of such a situation shouldn't be pleasant for you to contemplate.

Most defensive riding experts emphasize something else about staying

110

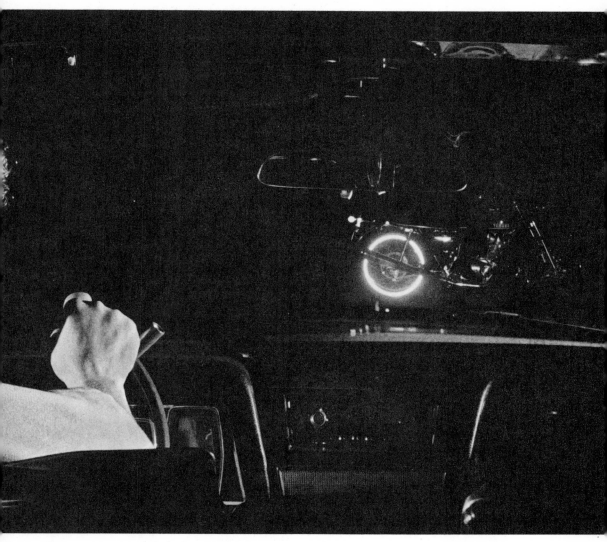

Extra care is needed if you ride at night. As this picture shows, the crossing motorcycle would be almost invisible to a driver if it wasn't for the reflective sidewall tire being developed by Goodyear.

Reflective tape molded into the sidewall of this Goodyear tire and incorporated into a rider's glove can provide extra protection for night riding.

in lane: you should stay in it, not ride between lanes. That's a suggestion that doesn't win many points with most newcomers to cycling—and quite a few veterans as well. After all, one of the nice things about a motorcycle is that it's compact transportation, compressed into a width only a few feet across. When traffic is slow or stalled, the argument goes, you don't have to wait around. Just edge into the space between the lanes and zip, you're off and running. But accident records bear strong evidence that saving a few minutes' time can prove expensive in doctors' bills. Someone may suddenly open a door to see what's holding up traffic or, even in slow-moving traffic, a driver may still see an opportunity to change lanes. The driver is looking for other large machines like his own four-wheeler, not a will-o'-the-wisp cyclist and, for you, the picture could end with a dull thud.

Freeway riding calls for considerably closer attention to efficient riding than normal street operation. Besides leaving a good stopping distance allowance, choice of lane is also important. Taking the center divider as the starting point, the number one lane is the one immediately to the right and is the fastest, lane two is second to the right and slower and so on. Engineering surveys by several bike builders indicate the safest lane for freeway riding is either number two or three, depending on whether it is a three- or four-lane highway.

Defensive riding is particularly crucial in bad weather, which has much more severe effects on a motorcycle performance than on most other vehicles. A rain slick street (or one made slippery by snow or sleet) causes a considerably greater reduction in traction for a bike than an automobile. At the same time that you have to worry more about keeping your own vehicle from skidding, you're also far more vulnerable to an accident caused by the loss in driving efficiency of a four wheeler.

An automobile driver has much less control over the car when streets are wet, and the car's braking ability is also degraded. This considerably increases the danger that an automobile traveling too close to you or coming on you unawares will hit you compared to normal road conditions. To all this is added the fact that the chance of an accident is increased by the degraded visibility for both cyclist and automobilist in bad weather.

The best thing for you to do when adverse weather hits is to stay off the streets. At the very least, you should move off the road for a time when

113

rain first starts to fall because it tends to distribute any oil or other lubricant on the road over a broader area. However, since the roadway is sloped to allow water to run off to the gutters, this hazard is removed after a while by the water's action. If a rainstorm hits, experience dictates you should move off the street, hopefully under some shelter, for a minimum of fifteen minutes to allow the rain to wash away the oil film. If it is a hard rain, you should wait longer, if necessary, until it slacks off. When this happens, head for home at a reduced speed.

Cold weather riding also calls for precautions. Besides dressing warmly, you should also move off the road at regular intervals to restore circulation. A little time in a warmer place or a hot drink will go a long way toward getting your nervous system back to top efficiency and thus minimize your decreased reaction time in cold weather. The fact that cold weather has this effect should be kept in mind when you have the urge to go faster than usual to try to reach the greater comfort of your destination. In cold weather, you're better off going slower than faster.

High winds can also cause you problems. They make it harder to maintain control over the bike whether you're going in a straight line or cornering. Your best approach, as for any bad weather condition, is to get off the road until conditions improve. If you don't do this, you should concentrate on keeping your bike under control. Hold on tighter and be ready to compensate for sudden changes in wind velocity. You should also lean forward to cut down on wind resistance.

Defensive riding calls for avoiding hazards whenever possible. Thus you should try to keep from riding behind a bus, truck, or other large vehicle. Obviously, such massive machines will block off your forward vision so that you may come on a pothole or other obstacle unexpectedly. Assuming you have a clear view ahead, you should make every effort to detect problems and to make provision for careful crossing of such things as railroad tracks, bumps and manholes, bridge grates, and so on.

When you come upon a tricky road feature or a puddle too suddenly to slow down, don't panic! Remember the proper technique as outlined by Yamaha experts, "hit it straight on, maintaining a constant speed, keeping a firm grip on your controls and riding in a semistanding position. Do not brake unless you can do so *before* you hit the object. If you must brake, use rear brake only and slightly. Raise your body slightly off the seat to maintain balance."

Some of the principles of cornering were discussed earlier. Besides knowing how to make the turn, you should also train yourself to do it without hazard. One point is to remember to give a turn signal sufficiently ahead of starting your turn. The law states you should give this signal 100 feet in advance, the same distance required for automobiles. Control of the bike is essential, so it's preferred that you use a turn indicator so you can keep both hands on the handlebars. If your turn indicator isn't working, you must use hand signals. These are the same as for an automobile: hand extended straight out to indicate a left turn, or at a right angle with the fingers pointed up for a right-hand one. However, once you're performing the turn, you should have both hands on the handlebars.

While you're waiting to make a turn, keep both wheels pointed straight ahead. The reason for this, the same as for a car, is so a bump from behind won't propel you into the path of oncoming traffic.

There are things you must consider if you want to take along a passenger. For one, it's not only dangerous, but illegal to carry a passenger on a bike not equipped for one. There must be seating space allotted on the bike and a second set of footpegs.

It's just as vital for your passenger to wear protective clothing as it is for you, including helmet, gloves, heavy shoes and boots. Once the passenger is dressed and ready he or she should wait until you've started the motorcycle before climbing on. (Similarly, the passenger should stay in place until the cycle is at rest with its engine turned off before dismounting.)

The passenger should hold onto you with both hands and have a good idea of what to do when the bike is moving. You should stress to your passenger the need for coordinating both your movements. The passenger must stay relaxed and not sit up stiff and straight when you're changing your body position for turns or other maneuvers. The cyclist, Yamaha points out, "must be aware of the effects of this added weight in terms of handling. Because of the added weight, always maintain adequate stopping distance between you and the vehicles in front of you." In other words, with a passenger, it's a good idea to add another few cycle lengths separation distance than that normally suggested for the solo rider.

Just as the preferred mechanical features of bikes differ for street and trail use, so do many of the riding precautions. As was indicated earlier, bikes have to be more ruggedly built for trail than for street use. Equally important for extended backcountry cycling is reliability. A trail bike should have systems that can go on for a great many hours without breaking down and everything should be as simple as possible from the standpoint of emergency repairs. Obviously, no matter how well a bike is engineered for reliability, its operating performance still depends on how well it's maintained. An important rule if you're an off-road riding fan is to take good care of all your equipment all the time and make detailed checkups of bike condition just before you go on any demanding trips.

Preferably you should stress preventive maintenance. You should be able to take a bike apart and put it back together again if you're a serious trail cyclist. Knowing what make a bike tick ensures that you can note many problems just from local riding that you can take care of before going into remote areas. That's doing it the easy way; you won't find it much fun trying to take something apart when the "work table" is a flat rock or a slippery patch of grass when the sun may be searing down or the rain pelting the ground. All in all, the maxim holds that an hour in the shop is worth three on the trail.

There are many other steps that will help ensure safe, comfortable trail riding. Having the proper dress is one of these. You want the standard array of items for bike riding mentioned earlier, but all of it from boots to helmets should be the strongest, most wear resistant obtainable to withstand the thorns, branches, flying dirt and stones of the countryside. Waterproofing is a must on all outside clothing.

A tear resistant riding suit is important; the Motorcycle Industry Council suggests using the canvas suits imported from England. A plastic raincoat, which has the advantage of folding into a small package, should be taken along. It can serve double duty, providing you with rain protection or a ground cloth for an emergency overnight stay. In the latter case, you can keep warm by placing a layer of dirt or pine needles on the raincoat. The layer does this by trapping your body heat when you're lying on top of it.

In the back country the password is "survival," and this calls for having adequate tools and spares and a compact "food kit." For that you might include such things as bouillon cubes, a compressed high energy food bar or two, and some packages of instant beverage. You should add

116

a waterproof matchbox so you'll have the makings for a cooking fire if needed.

The need for a comprehensive tool kit that will handle all the field needs of your machine has been noted. Besides the extras suggested earlier, other helpful items for trail use include a pocketknife; three-in-one screwdriver with common handle, large and small blades and Phillips shaft; a hand ax; and a chain-breaker. The latter can be vital if you need to replace a broken drive chain. It's all important that you take along several replacement chain links for such an emergency. Select a good knife with a variety of blades, including a spring-guard screwdriver. You'll find it handy in many ways, including treating injuries, cutting food, removing coatings from wire ends, making an improvised fishing rod, even blazing a trail through cutting notches in trees or stakes.

Some other spares you should cache somewhere on your bike include several spark plugs, a length of gas line, spare footpegs, an extra shift lever, throttle cable and clutch cable. For the last two, you should bring cables that already have been used on your bike so you're sure they will fit properly. Al Griffin (*A Buyer's and Reader's Guide to Motorcycles*) also recommends having a large supply of inner tube rubber bands:

"This is often better than baling wire for holding a falling-apart bike together because they won't work loose with trail bouncing. A series of them can be interlinked together to form flexible strapping long enough to hold even split gas tanks to the frame."

Consider taking a headlight bulb, fuses, a quart of gas and tire patches. In general, expert consensus is that trying to repair an inner tube in the field is a step of last resort. Bob Hicks' trail bike report for the Motorcycle Industry Council, for instance, states, "A tube is a waste; if your flat is a bad puncture, ride it out, it's easier." For a slow leak, he suggests having a can of tire inflator with sealant in your survival kit as the best answer. Another handy item is a 50-foot roll of mechanic's iron wire, which can be used for such varied things as holding on loose parts or as an impromptu fishing line.

Fastening on all the extra gear to the bike calls for some ingenuity. Trail riders don't like to have excess storage containers flapping in the wind, so the general approach is to fasten the spares, tools that won't fit into the regular tool compartment, and other items to the frame with friction tape, baling wire or even nuts and bolts.

If you're a trail rider, such normal backpacking items as a compass, wide-mouth canteen and a compact plastic tube tent should be part of your gear. Some small change for emergency phone calls also is a good idea. Though not absolutely necessary, it's worth taking along a map of the region you plan to visit. As an experienced backpacker knows, excellent maps are available for almost every section of the United States from the U.S. Geological Survey in Washington, D. C. Sometimes you can get good maps from local camping or mountaineering stores or they may be able to tell you where you can find these in your town or city.

After several off-road trips, you may come up with some additions of your own. To jog your memory for each journey, it might help to have a master checklist on the garage wall which you can consult, modify and study constantly when you're preparing for a trip. Without a list, the most experienced trail buff can occasionally omit a key item that can make a routine ride into a bone-wearying struggle. A motorcycle can bring moments of carefree, fast-paced movement through magnificent natural regions rarely disturbed by man, but it can become a heavy burden if you're 50 miles from nowhere and a tragedy entitled "the missing link."

That sort of situation points not only to the need for careful planning, but also the value of the buddy system. Every year there are a distressing share of stories about lone motorcyclists who get trapped by themselves in some remote wilderness or desert area. For the most part, searchers find these people in time. Sometimes the cyclist is unharmed, sometimes injured, occasionaly, though, the ending of the story is all too final. Survival rule number one for you, therefore, is never to go trail riding alone. With a buddy riding a second machine, if you find you're missing a tool or a spare part, your pal can supply it. If one of you is injured, the other can provide emergency aid and go back for help.

Even with a buddy or a group of fellow riders, if you're thinking clearly you'll stick to the trail. For one thing, keeping to a trail, even a long-forgotten out-of-the-way one, eliminates the chance of getting lost. Equally important, if you ride your bike off the trail there's more chance it may hit an obstacle and get broken. There's also the fact that you can cause irreparable damage to the ecology of the countryside. Destroyed vegetation and animal life all too often have been left in the wake of some cyclists. Such occurrences feed the outcry of forces that want to limit motorcycle use severely. That could lead eventually to keeping everyone, including yourself, from a lot of the good times of cycling.

To sum up, your motorcycle is a sophisticated, high performance machine that you should treat with respect. However, a review of the majority of considerations outlined in this chapter should convince you they are based on common sense and not difficult for you to do.

In sports, knowing the rules and abiding by them doesn't detract from the enjoyment, and it's the same for motorcycling. More so, in fact. You can disregard a tennis rule, dare a football official to mark off 10 or 15 yards if he catches you clipping or holding, or try to fool a baseball umpire with an illegal pitch, but ignoring the good sense maxims of motorcycling can lead to a very short riding career indeed.

INDEX

The Author

Irwin Stambler is an expert in the cycle and automotive field who has written many popular books for Putnam's. His most recent well-received book on wheels and wheelmen was *Here Come the Funny Cars*. Among his books are *Great Moments in Stock Car Racing, The Supercars and the Men Who Race Them, Automobiles of the Future,* and *Unusual Automobiles of Today and Tomorrow*. He lives with his wife and children in Beverly Hills, California.